The current problems facing society, whether they be economic, global warming or pressures of migration, are excessively discussed but this book considers the separate problems and sets out a realistic solution with a defined pathway. The cause and effects are considered based on the historical trail to the present unsustainable position in terms of current scientific and economic knowledge to asses the consequences that will inevitably follow. Although based on science, these are explained without the need for an academic background, in any discipline, with the solution justified in every aspect. The actions and dramatic changes in just the last half of the twentieth century have put the whole world environment at risk. The younger generation will have to resolve the resultant problems and this book is dedicated to them as it is their future that is in the balance.

Chapter 1
Background & History

Imagine setting off down a mountain stream, picking up speed and then sweeping into eddies, choosing to be carried downwards again, excited by the acceleration and adventure of new vistas around each bend. Imperceptibly the water flow grows, fed by hundreds of little streams until you are rafting down rapids dodging boulders and waves. The river has now cut a canyon, the sides are near vertical, daunting, and now stopping is nearly impossible. The raft hurtles on, carrying all aboard, there is no getting off, any one having second thoughts is caught struggling to keep afloat, never having time to think what lies ahead, being carried to the end. The momentum is self perpetuating but what does lie ahead is that either the river will flow calmly into a lake or it will cascade over a vast waterfall carrying all on board like lemmings to their deaths.

There is a fork in the torrent; a possibility that by concerted effort the raft can modify its course. The option appears even steeper and more perilous than the main path but logic implies that both paths lead to the same level; the steeper path is probably a better bet. Whether logic can be applied, whilst hurtling along trying to just stay afloat, is another matter.

This is where we find ourselves today. With society hurtling along the path that was never really planned with everyone trying to steer away from boulders and dangerous rapids, even the people steering have lost control and can do little more than avoid the immediate catastrophes that suddenly appear.

The momentum is such that there is no opportunity for considered planning; it just simply lurches from one potential disaster to the next.

This is the background to the fundamental question facing everyone, whether society is functioning for the benefit of every member or whether it has become a self-perpetuating giant that controls and drives us, but do we have the time or information to make a considered judgement? It has become an uncontrollable torrent, carrying everyone despite the majority being dissatisfied by their lifestyle and situation. The function of the various controlling bodies, whether governments or enormous multi-national corporations, is equally regulated by this system that has evolved not by design but by default.

This should be inconceivable as democracy is designed to retain the power in the hands of the majority and, at the end of the day, even the multi-nationals are controlled by their shareholders, which through the various trusts and pension plans spread the ownership widely across the population. The vast majority of the population are little better than slaves compelled to work long hours simply to survive. In theory there is choice, however, the reality is that in modern society every adult member of each family unit is pressurised into working continuously simply to maintain their standard of living.

The apparent inconsistency can only be rationalised by considering the fundamental functioning of the whole system. Modern society has evolved from the industrial revolution when mechanical power was utilised for the first time to assist and enhance our ability to work. The form of work is not in itself important but the use of external energy sources to provide goods, services and crops for consumption totally changed the balance of labour and the form of society.

In reality, the beginning of this change evolved thousands of years earlier when animals were first used for transport and farming. At this stage, crops were specifically grown, or land was set aside, for the production of food crops for the working animals. In essence the energy from the sun was captured and stored in animal fodder to ensure that sufficient energy was available throughout the year to enable the working livestock to function efficiently and productively.

This ability to capture the sun's energy in a regulated and planned way has enabled man to evolve from a hunter gatherer to our privileged position today. It is more normal to consider crops and foodstuffs as entities in themselves but their intrinsic value is in the energy captured from the sun, stored in the seeds or plants themselves. This energy storage can be modified and concentrated by keeping animals for food, either through dairy produce or simply as meat.

The question is, whether the success of mankind is the result of our intelligence and ability to build sophisticated societies or whether it is a direct result of our ability to control energy. Without the heat from fires, prehistoric man would have remained on a par with the other occupants of the planet, with the population and evolving society decimated by each harsh winter. Many animals collect the surplus of nature's bounty but if they cannot survive the climatic extremes then this is completely wasted, but once a species begins to beat the system, then continuing evolution becomes a possibility.

The growth of civilisations can be linked directly to their ability to provide food, both for the population and livestock. In societies where there was a surplus, the population grew and part of the working population could then be utilised to work in areas other than food production. These became the artisans and military of the ancient world, fed and clothed by an efficient and well managed agricultural base, providing the driving energy essential to continue the cultural and geographical expansion.

The energy providers were the landowners, while their workers cultivated the land to generate wealth and power for the owners. British feudal society was far from perfect but at least each individual worker could identify his local lord. The taxes paid were sufficiently high to ensure that the status quo was maintained and no worker or even tenant farmer could readily generate sufficient disposable wealth in his own right for him to achieve real independence. This had the effect of stabilising society, undoubtedly for the primary benefit of the landowners, but at the same time the delicate balance of the environment was maintained.

At this stage in human development, the energy system was totally sustainable in that all consumption was cyclic, with the waste products from consumption being returned to the system in the same proportions through absorption by the new crops. At the same time, the system was localised, based on individual farms and communities that provided for themselves as well as creating a surplus for sale in the adjoining towns. The only energy input was directly from the sun, converted entirely by photosynthesis in plants to the products required. There were both wind and water mills but the reality is that their source of energy is ultimately derived from the sun. This even applied to domestic heating, virtually entirely from wood fires, although in this case the cyclic period was extended to several years simply because of the time taken for trees to reach adequate size. In practice, the main building material both for houses and ships was wood therefore a significant part of the tree growth was retained for many years.

The effect of this is to hold the chemical compounds in the wood in suspended animation for many years by delaying the natural process of rotting and decomposition that would take place in a natural forest. Wood is a complex mix of hydrocarbons and by delaying the decomposition for decades the result is a reduction in the amount of carbon dioxide in the atmosphere. Wood is almost entirely hydrocarbon, which decomposes to carbon dioxide and water, with minute trace elements and a small amount of nitrogen, which is released either as nitrous oxide or as nitrates. As long as the quantity of wood undergoing decompososition - either by burning or natural decomposers - is balanced by the new growth, then the system remains sustainable and completely unchanged in the longer term.

Man can also influence this balance. If a 40 Kg floor joist is built into a house then this locks in over 30 Kg of carbon which on decomposition would add over 140 Kg of carbon dioxide to the atmosphere. This is a fairly average weight for floor structural timber used in the construction of dwellings, with a modern house using several tonnes of wood. Equally, if this is allowed to decompose then plants absorb the carbon dioxide and release the oxygen back into the atmosphere, while using the carbon for new plant growth.

On the other hand, every time we consume 40 kilos of hydrocarbon or fossil fuel, we create 140 Kg of carbon dioxide, which ends up in the atmosphere, and upsets the long-term natural balance of growth and decomposition. This happens directly every time we turn on the car or the central heating system both of which burn fuel, but it happens indirectly whenever the instantaneous power that we take for granted is used, every time we turn on the light switch, using electricity that has been produced in the main by burning fossil fuels. The vast numbers of individuals in the world today mean that the small amount of energy consumed by every light bulb is multiplied a billion times over. Everyone is concerned about environmental damage but because the numbers and the problems are so vast, there is a tendency to expect governments to resolve the problem, but the reality is, that the root cause is individual consumption.

A trip round the aquarium in Genoa paints a picture of a Mediterranean scene before human domination with lush indigenous hardwood forests cascading down the mountainside to the seashore. These forests were a mix of oak, chestnut, beech and so on and can still be found in small isolated pockets all across Europe. These forests not only provided us with a much more extensive ecosystem and diversity than the areas of pine forest that have in part replaced them, but they also created a deep bed of decomposing leaf matter under the canopy. A walk through a mature deciduous forest clearly demonstrates the extent and the depth of the rotting leaf matter which provides the habitat for the vast range of insect and fungal life forms which will be providing a medium of water retention. On the other hand, pine forests which are now predominant in Europe do not provide this sort of structure which makes them more susceptible to forest fires, leading to repetitive destruction. Hardwood forests provided, in effect, an enormous sponge covering the whole of Europe, retaining and regulating the water flow and largely eliminating soil erosion.

Mediterranean Europe was heavily forested at the beginning of the Roman Empire but the forests were systematically cut down to fuel the growing empire and replaced by fields for food crops. The Romans systematically expanded their empire, bringing with them improved technology to improve both crop yields and varieties but at the expense of major changes to the environment.

Each individual needs 2,000 calories (K Calories) every day in food to be adequately fed so that normal everyday tasks can be carried out. This is the equivalent of an energy input of 2.2 Kwh per day; the farmers must produce this both for themselves and for every other member of society. The expansionist programmes of civilisations originated from a need to expand their agricultural base to increase their food surpluses in order to maintain and enhance their society. In terms of energy management the Roman Empire can be considered as a natural progression from the earlier civilisations of the Greeks. The Romans, starting in Italy around 600 BC, evolved and expanded the area under their direct control to virtually the whole of Europe as we know it today, until 400AD. (A span of 1000yrs). Put into perspective, it is less than two hundred and fifty years since the American War of Independence and only 150yrs since the start of consumption of hydrocarbon fuels (coal & oil).

In practice, deforestation in Roman Europe for construction, especially of military ships, must have had the effect of a very minor increase in the carbon dioxide level in the atmosphere. The Romans had developed very clever and relatively efficient wood-fired heating for their villas and baths, resulting in an expanding demand for fuel wood. This demand was satisfied by continual expansion and consistent extensions into the European forests.

Unfortunately this also led to extensive soil erosion and loss of quality agricultural land. The recently discovered complete ships buried in the old Roman port of Pisa show the extent of the erosion taking place at the time. It appears that the whole harbour was swamped by floodwater, which left the docks and the ships in port, completely covered in silt to a depth of over two metres. The storms causing this flooding were undoubtedly unusual but the indisputable fact is that there was soil erosion on a massive scale; this must have resulted in much lower crop yields in subsequent years.

The fall of the Roman Empire is classically put down to general decadence and debauchery, usually visualised as sumptuous steam baths in sophisticated villas, but this was paralleled by the reduced productivity of the agricultural base by systematic over-cropping of the land and the destruction of the forests. In reality, their ability to capture and store the sun's energy was decreasing as the empire itself began to decay, it could be argued that this was the real reason for the breakdown of the empire.

The original dramatic growth of the UK economy started with the agricultural revolution, which provided a greater surplus of foodstuffs with a smaller farming population and freed a number of workers from the land. The newly available labour was the trigger for industrial growth, first fuelled by water and windmills. The radical change was the steam engine, which for the first time provided mechanical power, not tied to a river. In historical perspective, the first steam engines were operating by 1840 and Stevenson's first railway engine was made in 1860. The amount of power available was vast, measured in several Horse Power for each engine, and they worked anywhere where water was available and where it was practical to transport fuel. Initially they were fuelled by wood and the delicate balance of the environment was still being maintained, at least in theory, but the forested area was decaying.

But then there was coal, with a higher energy value and readily available throughout middle England.

The effect was dramatic. Within a few decades there were

new railway systems providing fast and reliable transport for people and goods. The factories expanded, producing steel in vast quantities to make even more efficient machines and the English economy bounded forward into a growth cycle that had previously been impossible. England was soon the most powerful nation in the world, maintaining and perpetuating a vast empire, and exporting their newfound expertise around the world by building railway and other systems.

The reality was that this growth was not due only to the increased knowledge or the new technology of machines, but was founded on an internal, readily available energy source. At this stage the coal mines in England were virtually all on or very near to the surface and the coal seams were very rich in good quality coal. It was there to be collected by anyone and, in just a few decades, a major industry evolved in the mining, sorting and transport of coal around the UK.

These changes were mirrored across Europe and major manufacturing areas evolved wherever there was a ready supply of coal and water.

Coal production in the UK (graph 1) shows the exponential growth in the century from 1850, from a new industry providing specialised fuel in the early years to a mass volume economic driving force, forming a major element of the British economy. The downturn in growth in the coal industry has traditionally been blamed on the availability of cheap oil-based fuel and natural gas but the reality is more that the cost of extraction of every ton of coal rose with every ton consumed. At the point of maximum production coal was still just competitive but in every subsequent year the cost per ton escalated to the point at which the coal industry could only be maintained by massive subsidies.

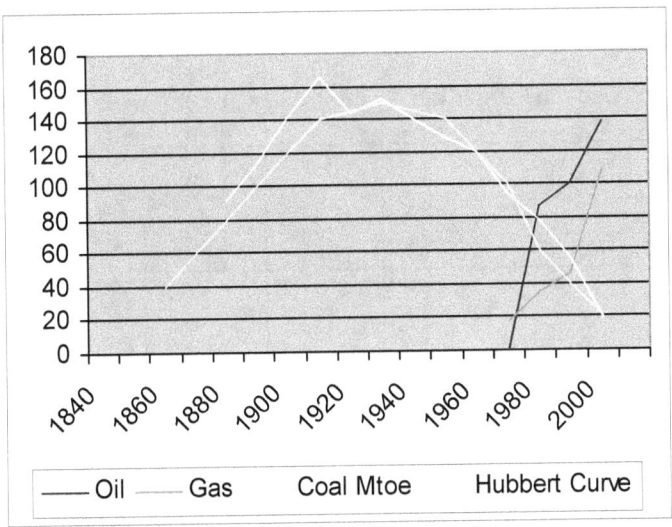

UK Energy Production

This is the fundamental point. Britain did not run out of coal, and there are still substantial reserves available in the UK but the system began to collapse because the cost of extracting the coal was pushing the prices of consumer goods out of the reach of the consumer. At this point in the cycle, demand exceeded supply, fuelling price rises, with the shortfall made good by imports. This could only result in a slowing of the economy as factories closed due to lack of demand for their products, leading directly to increasing unemployment. The subsidies provided directly to the coal and electricity generating industry helped to slow the process but they could never have been maintained against an ever-rising energy bill.

	Bread 1lb in p	Coal per ton in £	Property per 100m2 in £	Beef per 1lb in p
% Change in 100yrs	975	2000	1275	1650
% Change 1935-1975	860	2250	800	1167
1975	8.6	31.5	7000	70.0
1965	4.0	15.0	3208	32.0
1955	2.6	7.7	2567	16.0
1945	1.3	3.6	933	9.0
1935	1.0	1.4	875	6.0
1925	0.9	1.5	700	7.0
1915	0.6	1.4	700	6.0
1905	0.6	1.3	600	5.0
1895	0.5	1.2	600	4.5
1885	0.6	1.1	600	4.0
1875	0.8	1.5	510	4.0
1865	0.9	1.0	500	3.0
1855	0.9	0.9	450	3.0

The table shows that inflation is a twentieth century phenomenon and that the rise in coal prices is reflected in all other sections of the economy. This is despite the fact that oil was already available to provide an alternative and that energy demands by today's standards were low. A direct comparison of prices is confused by the various subsidies especially in relation to foodstuffs that tend to artificially depress the price. At the end of the day the consumers pay tax for the Exchequer for the subsidies, mitigating the benefit of the subsidies for all but the very poorest in society.

It is also clear from the costs of all items that prices did not rise significantly until the time of the 2nd World War but even in this period the rises were minor in comparison with the dramatic rises seen from 1950 to 1980. The effect is that goods costing £10 in 1975 would have cost only £1 in 1935.   This inflation has the effect of devaluing the currency which has a dramatic and devastating effect on those in society who are living on a just balanced budget. Those who have significant disposable income after paying for the essentials are still affected but they have the choice as to where their disposable income is allocated not whether they can afford heating or food. Those with real assets see the value effortlessly increasing over time and debts remain at the same numerical value whilst those with lower incomes and assets invariably see income growth lagging behind price increases.

Careful inspection of the rates of increase for various commodities indicate that rises in the price of raw energy precede and lead general price changes which seem to lag behind significantly. This was clearly demonstrated in the years following the 2008 financial crises where despite the resultant recession and a drop in oil price the overall inflation continued to be high for several years.

The growth in coal consumption was in part due to the expansion of the industrial base, burning coal for their own use, but also because coal was converted to other forms of energy more convenient for general use. Town gas was first supplied to London in *1850* to provide street and domestic lighting and over the following century, this gas was provided to many properties in England. The gas itself had one major defect in that it was composed of 20% carbon monoxide, which although combustible, is very poisonous. It is strange to think of supplying an extremely toxic gas to every houses in England, but this was a readily available form of energy used extensively for heating and cooking, up to the introduction of North Sea Gas in the 1960's.

It is worth noting that gas explosions were unheard of with Town gas and this was piped around major cities in galvanised steel tubes, prone to rusting and breakage, without any major accidents, despite one of the component gasses being toxic. The major component of coal gas is Hydrogen (over 50% but commonly 80%) and this was successfully used as a primary fuel source both in the UK and many other countries for at least a century. The reason explosions occur with hydrocarbon gas commonly known as natural gas, is because it is heavier than air and thus easily trapped inside buildings as an explosive mixture, only needing a spark to set it off. Conversely, hydrogen is the lightest gas available and will escape through the roof of a building, thus making explosive concentrations of gas impossible except in hermetically sealed containers.

The next major market for the coal industry was to supply coal to the electricity generating industry, who became the major consumer of coal in the UK. Electricity has the advantage of ease of use and the growth in electrical consumption has continued unabated since it first became available

As the use of coal escalated, the cities became blacker as the soot and acids in the air attacked the fabric of the buildings. London was plagued with pea soup fogs lasting several days on end where visibility was reduced to less than a couple of metres, people died from the fumes and soot was trapped in the air. In the end, restrictions were imposed on the burning of coal domestically, known as smoke control zones, but the population had cheap energy and the quality of life was perceived to be on the increase. The World Health Organisation estimates that 8,000 deaths annually were directly attributable to this pollution but there were doubtless many more affected in the longer term.

The effects of the resultant acid gases released into the atmosphere were not considered, they were not readily visible, and the damage to the water supply was ignored. The other invisible effect was the return to the current environmental system of the atomic carbon that had lain encapsulated since before the first dinosaur walked across the plains. The carbon released was not measured in Kg but in millions of tons. The same calculation applies to the weight of carbon dioxide produced as for the timber joist previously mentioned, but now there is no question of sustainability. In less than a century coal was burnt without any hesitation, releasing carbon hidden by nature for over 400 million of years.

In the South West of the United States, oil literally oozed out of the ground and as the coal industry in Europe careered to peak production this oil was starting to be extracted commercially. This was an even more convenient fuel, could be moved around in barrels, and could replace coal in virtually every case. In fact oil was even more versatile and soon the internal combustion engine began to replace the steam engine.

The American economy began to grow and by the end of the Second World War was the most influential economy in the world and still continuing to expand exponentially. This was not due to American business expertise or even the advantageous position they were in at the end of the war, but simply because they had a ready and virtually free source of energy available internally. This relationship between energy availability and the growth of civilisation is absolute and the former invariably leads to the latter.

The UK and Europe were saved from even more dramatic decline by the opening of the North Sea gas and oil fields in the early seventies. These just managed to plug the potential chasm looming up, as coal became more difficult and expensive to extract. Town gas was quickly converted to North Sea gas (methane) and the European economies managed to continue their push forward with only minor downturns. They could not realistically compete with the United States as, even from the outset, the cost of the oil was high due to the hostile environment of the North Sea, but they have survived.

Total world energy consumption keeps growing and growing with absolutely no prospect of dampening. Oil and Gas are convenient and readily available and do not have any of the visible pollutant effects of the coal era. For over a quarter of a century, specialists and scientists have been warning of the potential disaster looming ahead but, at the end of the day, convenience still prevails, helped by powerful lobbying and press coverage sponsored by the major energy companies. The desire to maintain our comfortable way of life has left the warnings ignored despite the scientific evidence. Our duly elected governments attend world conferences and heatedly argue minimal concessions to reducing the growth in greenhouse gas emissions.

Unfortunately, the governments are right, as any serious net reduction in greenhouse gas pollution with the current energy system would involve a dramatic change in standards of living for all. Idealists argue that we must make these changes to save the planet but realistically no government is prepared to enforce such a dramatic move and have any hope of remaining in power. Politicians, enthused with ideals immediately following an election, quickly become swamped by the administrative weight of government and all too soon the prospect of the next election tempers any radical changes.

History can teach many lessons but it is essential to place human history in perspective, both in geological terms and human terms. Consider that human society has evolved over a period of more than five thousand years from the ancient cultures in Mesopotamia to today. It is quite possible that we have seriously underestimated the timescale of human endeavour, but in any case, the period is less than fifteen thousand years. Even in relation to these timescales, the last century plays an insignificant part, a mere 10% of the span of the Roman Empire alone, but only within this period have significant changes been made to our environment. Whether these prove catastrophic or not, only time will tell, but the escalation of consumption of non-sustainable fuel sources without due consideration and planning is irresponsible.

Life on Earth has existed for over 400 Million years and over that period the two essential envelopes for existence, the sea and the atmosphere, have evolved into the environment we know today. Since humans became dominant, the changes have mainly been imperceptible, until the last century is considered. In reality, the significant and measurable changes due to human activity have all occurred in the last half-century.

Consider strolling along the touchline of a football pitch, at the starting goal line the dinosaurs have just become extinct and the few remaining are competing with the mammals. Towards the half way line the massive herds of roaming herbivores munch their way across the plains with a vast diversity of other, both small and large mammals, inhabiting the countryside. Well across the second half the first upright mammals can be seen and these slowly evolve into the human beings we know today. These appear just before the end goal line but now you need to kneel down with a magnifying glass. Well into this 5cm thick goal line, about a centimetre from its end, the beginnings of human civilisation can be seen. The thickness of the last blade of grass, about 0.2mm thick, represents the 20th Century in which we have changed the atmosphere and polluted the sea by sudden and excessive consumption of coal and oil deposits, which were laid down even before we started our walk.

In geological terms, these changes are instantaneous and could well be interpreted as a sudden natural disaster, however, the simple reality is that these are not planned or even calculated but simply the result of greed. The growth and continuation of society depends on the availability of energy but it is only in the 20th century that non-sustainable energy sources have been consumed.

The hypothesis is that the growth of civilisation is fundamentally tied to the availability and control of energy. Whether this is the Roman Empire tearing round to capture the sun's energy and valuable crops or the more recent availability of coal and oil is irrelevant. Growth is inexplicably linked to the supply of energy and the collapse is equally as linked to the downturn in the supply. Unless society evolves a new energy regime very quickly then we are almost certainly heading for a major depression which will make the downturn in the 1920's no more than a small appetizer.

It might seem inappropriate, or even conceited, to start with a potted history, and very selective potted history at that, of civilisation but it is essential to completely understand all the background to the problem. If the full extent and timescale of the current system is not understood, then the potential for making incomplete or erroneous deductions is considerable.

The fact is that the planet was a sustainable system until the mid nineteenth century and that even at the start of the First World War, the system was still basically in balance. It is only in the period from 1950 that human activity has destroyed this balance with the dramatic and still increasing consumption of fossil fuels.

Chapter 2
Now

There are many books and research papers detailing the current energy use in relation to levels of pollution, estimates of growth in demand and the looming disaster of the world running out of energy. It is almost impossible to sift through this mountain of information and deduce a clear and unambiguous picture of the effect on the delicate global ecosystem but it is clear that most informed writers believe we are headed towards very troubled waters in the near future.

The current level of energy use each year is over 9,500 mtoe (million tons oil equivalent) or 114,000 Twh (Terra Watt Hours), which breaks down to 1.8 tonnes of oil (about 1,700 litres) for each and every person on the planet. Less than 6% of this is produced from renewable sources and about the same globally by nuclear fuel, with over 75% directly from oil and coal. The difference is Biomass, which is largely wood burning for domestic use, predominately in the Third World.

Energy use is split between the developed and developing world verses the Third World, with the developed countries using about seven times that of the Third World whilst the developed population is only a seventh. This is one of the major areas of concern as development at present leads to dramatic increases in consumption and thus convergence. If even part of the Third World increased their consumption to the current levels in Europe then the world energy market would more than quadruple. It would almost certainly become unstable and the consequential effect on the planet's environment would be disastrous. Already, the effect of limited growth in China and the Pacific Rim appears to have pushed world energy demand to very near maximum world production of oil. The population of China alone will push consumption over the possible production limits if their consumption increases to a third of that in Europe.

As the Chinese economy was growing at an annual rate of up to 20% this is not an academic question. The reality is that the problem is looming over the next few years and even with the current slowdown in Chinese growth they are still growing four times faster than the developed world.

In Europe we consume the equivalent of 6 Kw per person continuously; this is six electric fires on every day throughout the year, non stop. This seems ridiculous but if the numbers are broken down in terms of personal use then the reality becomes apparent and this is for every individual including children

Industry accounts for a third of all energy used in the UK, The other two thirds are for domestic, transport & commercial use. These latter two are no more than the provision of goods and services demanded by individuals in society for their own consumption. It is clear from the above that it is the sum total of the individual usage that directly consumes the energy. Industry produces the products required by society so it is pointless to blame pollution and excessive energy use on industry as if it was some sort of goliath steaming away for its own benefit.

We must accept responsibility for the current position as individuals. A single light bulb cannot be blamed for melting the ice caps at the poles but one less light in every home would have an effect.

At present we are burning 7,200 mtoe annually in crude oil, gas and coal and this is steadily increasing. These reserves are finite and will thus run out at some stage but it is probably realistic to assume that the oil will last up to the middle of this century, with coal lasting a further few hundred years. However, although there might well be oil and gas reserves, production from these fields will fall away as the reserves are depleted and the coal that is remaining on the planet will become progressively more expensive to extract. The world energy demand can be satisfied for the foreseeable future but at what cost, both in pure monetary terms and in damage to the environment.

From an environmental point of view the outlook is bleak; all the carbon hidden away for well over 300 million years will be returned to the system in less than a century. We are already measuring negative effects and carbon dioxide levels will at least double again in the next fifty years. Our cities suffer from damaging pollution, choking the population in bad weather conditions, yet still causing illness throughout the year.

The measurable effects of climate change are now a regular feature of press and media comment, but the simple fact is that the ice caps are melting at both the poles, the glaciers in the mountains are disappearing and the perma-frost in the tundra's is melting. These are not the opinions of ideological scientists but the result of detailed measurements by dozens and dozens of researchers across the globe while systematically noting the changes to our environment. We can measure specific changes which have taken place but we are unable to generate a definitive and non-contentious projection of exactly what would happen next and over what time scale.

In the Carboniferous period, up to around 300 million years ago, the thriving plants and organisms gradually reduced the carbon dioxide levels in the atmosphere from over 80% to the trace levels that were below 0.03%, we know today. Measurements from air bubbles trapped in ice flows have been analysed and compared with temperatures over the past 160,000 years. Over that period there is a clear correlation between greenhouse gas concentrations and temperature. The carbon dioxide levels have varied between 0.018 %, corresponding to the ice ages and 0.028% in the last warm period immediately prior to the beginning of the industrial age. This level has now increased to 0.035% and more that half of this increase has taken place since 1960. In 2016 this was measured at 0.04% which represents a 60% increase since the Second World War. The intergovernmental panel on climate change (IPCC) concludes:
In terms of observed change, there has been a real but irregular increase in mean surface temperatures of 0.3 to 0.6 c over the past 100 years, a marked but irregular recession of the majority of mountain glaciers and the margins of the Greenland ice sheet, and a rise in sea level of between 1 and 2 mm per year.

(Houghton et al., 1990)

The environment is so complex that even our best computer models can only make a broad approximation of the effect of the changes we are making to the system. We are incapable of predicting the precise stage at which pollution levels become critical to the balance, therefore resulting in drastic changes in the environment. These are likely to be significant rises in sea levels and even more violent and unpredictable weather patterns across what would remain as dry land.

The ecosystem appears to be dynamically stable so that any changes are naturally corrected. This is much like the wheels on a bicycle acting as gyroscopes, inherently rotating in the same plane so that any wobbles are resisted by the wheels momentum and a natural reaction is created tending to reverse the instability. This does not prevent a cyclist falling, if the push is too great the bicycle becomes unstable and an immediate crash occurs. In the same way the earth is stable and natural. Cyclic corrections will smooth out any instability but at some stage this will cease to be true and disaster will follow. The problem is that we have no idea or reasoned assessment of at which point the instability will be reached but the consensus among meteorologists and scientists is that a mean rise in temperature of between 1.5 and 2 degrees will be the point of instability. But it is now accepted that we have passed the 1 degree rise by 2015 and this is measured on the same basis that would have accepted a rise of 0.25 degrees in 1990. This is an annual rise of 0.15 degrees leading to the conclusion that we will reach the critical point from mid 2018.

The world's population, surprisingly, is mainly located in the coastal areas and even a change in sea level of just one meter would displace millions of families. The result would be even higher population densities and even less viable land to provide the crops and food. Subsequently, it is quite likely the world would be plunged into an ice age as the main ocean currents, notably the Gulf Stream, ceased to flow. The result would be catastrophic for the developed world and quite possibly the whole human race.

The effects are clear with coral reefs dying across the world's oceans and individual species becoming extinct: all a direct result of human activity.

It seems a contradiction that global warming could, very quickly, lead to an ice age. The reasoning is that the Gulf Stream flowing from the Caribbean across the Atlantic and into the North Sea could stop flowing. The driving force for this current is the sinking of the water mass in the northern North Sea due to its high salt concentration making it heavier than the surrounding arctic waters. If global warming melts the ice caps and increases the rainfall in northern Europe, then this fresh water will dilute the salt concentration. If the Gulf Stream did stop flowing then the whole world's weather patterns would suddenly change, and within a few years, permanent ice would extend to below Paris. The salt concentrations in the North Sea have been measured and have fallen consistently and significantly in recent years.

The current environmental disaster as a direct result of human activity can only be halted by dramatic reduction in all pollution levels, predominantly carbon dioxide, and the return to energy sources that are truly sustainable. This is equally true even if you concur with the optimists today who believe that the environmental changes are containable in at least the medium term.

Much is made of Carbon Capture and there is no doubt that the natural world has the ability to adsorb carbon dioxide and to recycle this into growth in all organisms. Even at the current rate of UK hydrocarbon fuel usage it is possible to plant sufficient new trees so that after a few decades their growth would compensate for the extra human pollution. The conflicts are two fold: firstly the time taken to start to balance the pollution and secondly all the prime agricultural land in the UK would have to be turned over to forest. This would simply eliminate food production. Unfortunately the same calculation applies across the whole of the developed world.

Climatic change to more violent weather patterns can be sustained, especially in temperature-controlled dwellings, but both floods and even short periods of drought cause devastation to agricultural production. Most major river systems in Europe were flooded in the period from October 2002 to April 2003 and this, combined with late cold weather, seriously damaged food production. This was immediately followed by very dry and hot conditions, with drought affecting central Europe and resulting in further damage to the farming industry and tens of thousands of hectares being destroyed by forest fires across Europe, from Portugal to Italy.

The simple fact is that the significant and dramatic physical changes that we can measure are a direct result of global warming. It is now accepted that global warming is caused by greenhouse gas emissions and that the concentrations are increasing. Human activity is responsible primarily for the increase in carbon dioxide levels. The reality is that additional methane is also being produced, both by human activity and as a consequence of the warming effects in the atmosphere. The combination of these two can only lead to an escalation and acceleration of the climatic changes.

There has been considerable academic argument about the causes, extent and effect of human activity on the planet. The many scientists involved have considered this from the viewpoint of their own specialist fields with the result that we have innumerable theories, with as many assessments of the effects both in the short and long term.

Scientists approach things from an essentially academic point of view and analyse the quantifiable events in their specific field to understand the processes involved. Engineers are trained to find cost-effective solutions to specific problems but understanding and utilising the knowledge searched out by the scientists. It is critical that the problem is fully understood so that the solution actually resolves the real issue. Both engineers and businessmen must now apply their skills to finding workable solutions.

This does not in any way detract from the research already completed which has been essential to providing the background data and concepts needed to find real solutions.

It is individual demands that are the cause of Global Warming and unless this consumption is radically altered, very quickly, to virtually eliminate the greenhouse gas production, we could well find ourselves living in a very hostile and unstable world.

Chapter 3
Oil & Fuel

We can predict the exponential increase in oil costs as we pass the critical peak production point. This has been shown clearly with the continued mining of coal deposits in the past and was clearly demonstrated in 1970 with the oil crisis. This was related more to the USA surging past peak production levels with the cost of oil from these wells suddenly exceeding market price than any arbitrary price increase by OPEC. There is no doubt that the other oil producers jumped on the USA's fall from predominance for both economic and political motives but the fundamental change was that the USA was no longer self sufficient or the biggest producer in the world.

Jeremy Rifkin, in his book The Hydrogen Economy, provides a very clear picture of the current state of the oil industry and predicts into a very narrow time span the effect on the world energy market. His argument that world production will peak before 2010 based on a reasoned approach to oil reserves, past consumed production and potential demand has to be taken seriously. The additional reserves available by both Fracking and extracting oil from Tar deposits can slightly extend this prediction but only by a decade at best.

The thesis is that production follows a bell-like curve which starts slowly, and then rises rapidly as demand increases but slows towards the peak. The curve then mirrors the rise as production falls away to zero. This model, known as the Hubbert Bell Curve, was produced in a paper in 1956 outlining peak USA production between 1965 and 1970, but was considered unrealistic and unsound in the heyday of USA production. History proved not only the validity of the model but confirmed the prediction was accurate.

When a reserve is first tapped there are no initial customers and the production easily exceeds demand. As the consumers come on stream the demand rises but the production can easily be increased to keep all satisfied. At the peak point production starts to fall away but demand is still increasing steadily and this scenario can only lead to escalating prices.

- M King Hubbert for Shell Oil Company 1956

This curve appears to mimic the rise and decline of British coal production, Graph 1 , but more worryingly the UK oil and gas production appears to have peaked between 1999 and 2000. Oil production fell from 150.2 Mtoe in 1999 to 127 in 2002. Gas production was at 108.3 Mtoe in 2000 but down to 103.6 in 2002 and was further reduced in 2003. It is clearly too early to be definitive but it appears that North Sea gas and oil fields could well have already passed the point of peak production which will have devastating effects on the European economies. British Gas announced a 12% increase in domestic gas prices in the summer of 2004 sighting the general increase in wholesale gas price as the cause but this can only realistically reflect a supply and demand imbalance.

The Shell Oil Company has announced a major reduction in declared reserves in their 2004 annual report, and refused to confirm that there will be no more in the future. It is arguable that most of the "oil reserves" are significantly overstated at the present time as discussed at length in Rifkin's' Book. It is simply that Shell has bitten the bullet to now reassess their real reserves rather than simply allowing the figures to be carried forward for yet another year. By early 2005 Shell had reduced the declared reserves by a third of the total shown in their 2002 annual report. This was a shrewd financial move as oil prices had moved upward in the two financial years by in excess of a third resulting in the monetary value of the reserves remaining virtually static. The current estimates of the probable life of the remaining oil reserves become very questionable if this is typical of the industry.

It is realistic to accept that from 2006, the cost of oil will increase annually at around ten percent over the prevailing rate of inflation. It is probable that we have already passed the critical level and that the rise in crude taken over the last few years is not so much a market fluctuation, but the beginning of the steady increase in crude oil prices. If this is the case and the cycle has passed its turning point then we can only look forward to continuous increases in fuel costs. The outcry in 2001 from motorists and hauliers in the UK at fuel increases clearly demonstrates the speed at which frustration will boil over into militant action. If fuel continues to escalate at even a few % above inflation, the price will double in just over five years.

In 2001 the oil price was fluctuating around the $30 a barrel and this has moved steadily up to summer 2004 when the price has hit $50, a 50% increase in only three years. This trend continues with the price over $62 in mid summer 2005, highlighting the inescapable fact that crude oil has doubled in price in less than three years. It is generally accepted that a significant factor for the invasion of Iraq was to stabilise oil prices (at below $30 a barrel) and this has clearly failed. Analysts are now blaming this sudden increase in world oil price on increased demand from the developing nations especially in the Pacific Rim. Blame is not an issue, the simple fact is that current oil production can only just supply the demand even with Saudi Arabia pushing up their production to minimise the effect. Unless major changes are implemented then demand will continue to escalate whilst supply remains static and this can only lead to even further fuel price hikes.

What is personally reassuring but in real terms simply frightening is that since this scenario was written in 2004 it has proved accurate and real. The financial crisis in 2008 and the subsequent crash in the world economy resulted in significant falls in output and consequential falls in demand for energy. The apparent stability in energy prices from 2009 to 2012 are simply consistent with a shrinking world economyt since the slow down but now consistent return to numerical growth in most developed economies there has been a paralleled rise in raw energy prices.

The current oil production is largely located in countries with different ideological backgrounds and political systems to the major consumers. A significant proportion of these are politically unstable with majority of the major ongoing conflicts within these same areas. In reality many of these conflicts are promoted either directly or by covert political activities of the major consumer nations so it is hardly surprising that many of these producing areas are essentially hostile to the Western Powers.

There is a reasonable probability of a serious cut in oil supplies due to political instability resulting in escalating war or a change in control of major oil producers. This indeterminate risk will always be there whilst ever the West is dependent and aggressive towards producing nations and the effect on prices could be catastrophic.

Modern society is based on a ready low cost supply of energy, primarily in the form of oil and gas which account for over 80% of the energy used in the advanced economies. This dependence on an energy source which is outside their geographic and political control is potentially unstable and in a world economy where the demand already matches the production there are likely to be radical changes within these economies.

Private cars could be eliminated from the equation, but this would involve a major sociological change, which would be resisted probably to the point of collapse. More significantly, this would lead to the termination of a major world manufacturing industry with knock on effects in all the component manufacturers causing a significant increase in unemployment. The traditional market balance between supply and demand would be strained in every sector as product costs rose at a time when incomes were already straining to cope with the increased personal energy costs. The motor industry has declined steadily for at least the last decade and it seems that every year another manufacturer is pushed out of business. The trend of declining car sales and smaller cars reflect both consumer confidence and the general lack of disposable income available. The result is that consumers change their vehicles less frequently and tend to spend less in real terms on private transport.

The economies are now so interdependent that any major shift in manufacturing has knock on effects throughout the world. The phasing out of the motor industry over the next decade would destabilise the developed economies to such an extent that the world would almost certainly be plunged into a major depression. Unfortunately the whole system is based on confidence and at the point where either consumers or investors become disenchanted, then the bubble simply bursts. The momentum of the system continues to drive the economy forward ignoring the strains and visible cracks until the sudden point of collapse.

Every sector will be affected; however agriculture is realistically the most important. Modern industrial farming relies heavily on fuel to drive the equipment and manufacture the chemicals supposedly necessary to ensure a quality crop. It is already questionable whether the cost, in energy terms, of the chemicals in addition to the fuel used to manage the farms, is viable. The useable energy from the crops is already less than the input energy from our precious resources despite the free sunlight. Industrial farming has produced dramatic increases in yields in the short term, but these soon fall off and need higher levels of chemicals every year to maintain yields thus causing increases in pollution. It is now apparent that the older more traditional methods give consistent, if slightly lower, yields but over extended time periods.

The environmental pressure groups, notably WWF, have campaigned for improved regulation for chemicals used in agriculture but the governments are hesitant to ban products. This is no doubt in part due to pressure from lobbyists for the manufacturers but there is also an underlying fear that if agriculture were adversely affected then the subsequent problems would be politically destabilising. The problems with cattle production in Europe demonstrate both the sensitivity of the population to problems with the food chain but more significantly, we have industrialised the food production to such an extent that any problem is rapidly transmitted throughout the system.

European farming is heavily subsidised but despite this the farmers are certainly not reaping in huge returns but generally just managing to survive. This is a fundamentally dangerous position because without food then society will certainly be radically altered. It is the sustained food production that provides the driving force for any growth as it has been since before Roman times. The use of mechanical plant has reduced the agricultural workforce at the cost of the industry becoming a major pollutant directly by the use of fuels and indirectly by the industrial factories producing the chemicals used for herbicides, pesticides and fertilisers. In energy terms, agriculture in the developed world is not viable simply because the energy in the products, both grain and meat, is less or at best comparable to the total input energy used in their production. Additionally, in simple financial terms, without the current subsidies, each farmer would have to input capital every year to maintain production, which would clearly not happen, therefore the farming industry would either collapse or food prices would be forced up to several times their current levels.

The rising fuel prices will damage the developed economies in the first instance, leading to steadily increasing unemployment coupled to rising prices, which no increase in inflation will mitigate. While fuel costs continue to ever increase in real terms, then the pressure on prices will automatically continue and this is an ongoing cycle, which can only be resolved by utilising an alternative energy regime.

The analogy with the collapse of the Roman Empire, and virtually all the other lost civilisations, could well give a realistic historic example of the current direction society is heading in. The argument proposed is that the fall of the Roman Empire was brought on by the elimination of their ability to capture and store the incoming sun's energy because their agricultural system became less effective. In reality the only energy available to their society was reduced and this quickly led to the collapse of the whole Empire. Unless current oil use is radically altered then pollution and financial costs will continue to climb.

It is always difficult to accept that a global problem stems directly from the choices of each individual. The fact is that it is the sum total of individual energy consumption that is the direct cause of all the environmental pollution. If each individual refuses to modify their energy use then consumption will continue to escalate and either economic collapse or environmental disaster or both will be the inevitable result.

The conclusion is that oil prices will continue to escalate at over 10% annually until such time as the system simply becomes overstretched and confidence fails resulting in a major world depression.

There are two fundamental additions to these conclusions; the first is that energy consumption in the developed countries accounts for most of overall energy use. The bulk of the world population still utilizes minimal energy and as these populations aspire and move towards higher energy use for domestic and transport facilities then the overall problems escalate to catastrophic proportions. This alone could shorten the timescale to find solutions from a decade to no more than a couple of years.

The second element is that the developed world's absolute dependence on available energy leaves us in the position where any failure of the energy supply results is complete collapse of society. This collapse would result in major reductions in population due in part to modern society's current inability to survive in inclement weather with no energy combined with famine that would be caused by inability to transport and preserve food supplies as these are no longer available by localized production for the whole of the population.

In order to comprehend the current absolute dependence on readily and instantaneously available energy the history becomes both relevant and frightening. In the ten thousand years of evolution of human society up until 1850 AD energy use was fundamentally, if not absolutely, sustainable and there had been no significant effect on the world's oceans or atmosphere.

In the century from 1850 to 1950 AD the use of hydrocarbon fuel started, initially as coal and later combined with oil. This utilization of stored energy fueled the industrial revolution and the dramatic changes in technical advanced machines and industry. The parallel improvements in both living environments and medical advances have increased life expectancy. The result was a steady and continuous population growth in societies that were directly benefiting from these improvements. This growth in the UK has seen population rise from under 40 million to over 60 million, a 50% rise, since 1900 and this expansion is consistent across the developed world and higher in less developed regions.

At the end of the second world war energy use per person, taken as an average, had dramatically increased to the extent that overall consumption of hydrocarbon fuel had grown by a factor of three times over the century.

In the next fifty years from 1950 energy consumption mushroomed exponentially with overall consumption rising to the levels that we see today causing environmental changes and financial instability.

It brings to mind the panting lemming turning to his running mate, " I am not convinced that jumping over the cliff will necessarily improve my quality of life"

Chapter 4
Generation

Reliance on hydrocarbon fuel must be ended and the replacement fuel must be truly sustainable, without greenhouse gas emissions. Most agree with this, as long as the alternative maintains every individual's current standard of living, with no added financial burden. This is human nature.

Gas, oil and coal will continue to be used while they are readily available despite the pollution, simply because each individual cannot accept personal responsibility for the problem, and will certainly not compromise personal lifestyle simply for the idealistic benefit of the world. Only when an alternative is generally available at comparable cost will there be a significant and permanent reduction in hydrocarbon fuel consumption.

There are potentially only three sources of energy available that could possibly provide this alternative; nuclear, geothermal and solar.

The first extracts energy from controlled nuclear fission inside power generation plants. The miniscule loss of matter during these reactions is converted to energy, which is used to make superheated steam to drive the turbines. The energy output achieved when matter is destroyed is dramatically high, so the quantities of fuel utilised are relatively small even for major generating plants. There is no argument that these plants do produce clean electricity in terms of greenhouse gas production but there is also a proven risk that even the slightest loss of control can lead to major nuclear accidents. The results of the Chernobyl accident clearly demonstrate the potential risk at every plant. The nuclear industry now promotes its safety and design advances arguing that these plants were now safe and the only solution to the looming problem. Then the tsunami in Japan showed their real vulnerability and the disastrous impact when problems occur. This was the worst to date but by no means the first; it is simply a question of time before there is another major disaster.

The unit cost of the energy produced appears to be very competitive as long as no account is taken of the cost of decommissioning these plants when they reach the end of their practical life. This financial burden, combined with the problem of the disposal of the used fuel rods and the contaminated material used within the plant, makes this form of power generation impractical, too expensive and only a valid choice if there were no realistic alternative. As oil supplies escalate in price, the governments around the world are now conditioning the population to accept that massive nuclear plants to provide the only possible alternative.

This policy inherently accepts that fossil fuel supply will very soon be out of the reach of the majority, either due to dramatic price increases or environmental collapse. This is despite a constant assurance by national institutions, that there is no energy crisis or energy problem looming in the immediate future. The nuclear solution does however provide continuity of centralised generation maintaining political control which therefore perpetuates the existing system.

The development of fusion reactors would provide a realistic alternative and these would have no residual radiation. At present, the development has only enabled test reactions to be maintained for short periods but with substantial research and funding an operational generator is possible within fifty years or so. The first prototype plants are now under construction but it will still be decades before these can be developed into viable systems.

In essence, this involves creating a mini sun within artificially controlled plasma joining isotopes hydrogen atoms together. The result of this reaction is identical to that which takes place within the sun and the energy would be given off as high intensity light. The reaction converts a miniscule proportion of matter into energy, so this reaction can be considered to be both sustainable and non-polluting. This is a viable way forward but it is unlikely that the technical problems will be resolved before the world energy price increases causes a breakdown in the current structure.

Once second phase operating plants become a reality these would be a viable solution to provide power to major cities as these can be realistically built locally. Again it would be realistic to have these operated and managed by each city administration. As these authorities would also be responsible for granting consent to construct and the output would be for the benefit of the city it would seem reasonable for control and management to be vested with them

Geothermal energy is the heat energy retained in the earth's molten core which can be tapped, by passing water into the core and using the superheated steam produced, to drive steam turbines. These have a very high initial cost and realistically have to be located in areas of the world where the molten magna is close to the surface. These areas have, by their location, a high risk of earthquakes and volcanic eruptions making the plants vulnerable to damage. Geothermal plants do however produce environmentally friendly electrical power and where geographically practical, do provide a viable way forward.

In 1978 Bragi Arnason, professor of chemistry at Reykjavik University, proposed that Iceland could be a fossil fuel free zone by 2030 relying entirely on renewable resources for energy. His proposal involved hydrogen as the primary energy reserve and used as a fuel, completely replacing hydrocarbon fuel in the country. His ideas were dismissed as crazy and his hope that Iceland could be fully converted by 2030 is proving overly optimistic.

Today this crazy fantasy has now become a government backed opportunity in partnership with major companies, including among others Daimler –Chrysler & Shell, who are actively working to transform his ideals into a reality. The current programme is that Iceland will become a hydrogen society within the next 30 years. The use of geothermal energy sources makes the design complicated and large scale, with long construction times. The result is that the changeover is slow and requires massive capital investment in both the generating plants and the hydrogen production units.

Three hydrogen fuel cell buses were introduced in October 2003, plus the construction of a refuelling station, delivering hydrogen to the energy bottles located on the roofs of the buses. It is planned to begin renewing the Icelandic fishing fleet using fuel cells from 2015, and this one action will return the fishing industry to a profitable industry.

Currently, an extremely high proportion of the fish catch value is simply utilised to pay for the gasoil burnt by the vessel whilst at sea, resulting in a low added value to the fishing catch. Iceland has no natural oil reserves so all the fuel oil is imported from the world market with the result that the Icelandic fishing fleet's net benefit to the Icelandic economy is immediately slashed by over 50% simply to pay for the oil imports. If the hydrogen is produced locally from renewable resources then this lost value is immediately returned to the Icelandic economy and then the added value from fishing is more than doubled. The distribution of this added value will be determined by a combination of government policy and market forces, but the indisputable fact is that the whole of the wealth from each fish catch will all be for the benefit of Iceland society.

Iceland has a history of finding innovative and new energy sources, opting for geothermal and hydroelectric power whilst the rest of the world was rushing down the nuclear path. At present, they estimate that they have only tapped 16% of their country's' available renewable resources leading to the conclusion that Iceland could become the "Kuwait of the

North" supplying hydrogen to the rest of the world. It is also a closed system, making it easy to conduct real scale development of new technology because if it goes wrong, it is less difficult to fix according to Arnason (not the professor but the minister in charge of the program).

The preceding options require major capital investment in large scale generating plants, which logically result in operational management by large multi-national corporations either by themselves or in association with central government. In effect, development along these lines perpetuates the centralised power systems already in place. Power relates to both generated energy and political control, the two of which are inextricably intertwined in modern society.

The right to breathe is taken for granted, and remains both untaxed or controlled. It is equally arguable that we have the right to free and unencumbered use of the sun's energy as this arrives on earth every day and impinges on our personal environment. Centralised power collection and distribution is inconsistent with the nature's structure. An oak tree has thousands of leaves acting as mini solar collectors and the survival of the tree is ensured by every single leaf but not dependent on any one leaf or group. This applies to every plant and their survival is a result of diversity and multiplicity. It would be wise to learn from nature and match our societies to ensure both diversity and a multiplicity of sources.

Solar energy arrives on the earth's surface as sunlight at the continuous rate of 173,000 TW, whereas the rate of world primary energy consumption is approximately 13 TW continuous power equivalent. In other words, the amount of solar energy received every year, or day, is 15,000 times the worlds current energy use. The issue is therefore not whether there is an alternative energy source, but whether we have the ability or wish to utilise and control just a small part of the power available to us.

Solar energy drives the water cycle, evaporating water from the seas to form clouds which produce rain and hence the rivers. Part of this energy can be converted to electricity in hydro electric stations and around 40,000 TW of the incoming energy is absorbed by this cycle of evaporation and precipitation, therefore making it theoretically possible to recover 4TW or 30% of the world's energy use from this source. This figure would be dramatically increased to at least 50% if micro generating stations were considered.

Current thinking leads to major hydroelectric installations, usually involving major dams and massive local infrastructure changes by relocation of villages and roads. These cause changes to nature's evolved balance, altering the local ecosystem and invariably leading to visual pollution by the installation itself and the new electric pylons carrying the generated power away. This again essentially maintains power generation in large centralised plants linked to the national grid distribution system, thereby maintaining both energy power and political power control within the centralised system.

The essence of future generation must involve free flow

capture rather than modifying the environment to suit human needs. Solar energy arrives on each section of the earth's surface every day and when this is converted by panels into electrical energy this production is only related to the incoming energy from the sun. This is the essence of a free flow energy system where the available energy is collected as and when available and is totally independent of human needs and usage. The same logic applies to wind turbines and this philosophy must be utilised in the construction and use of both tidal and hydro generating systems.

Micro plants can be designed to utilise only part of the water flow, thus maintaining the rivers natural course with the extra generated power used to produce hydrogen for transportation either through underground pipelines or by vehicles. Water mill power was common before 1900 and any old map will show every river with small millponds and millraces providing power to the local industry. It was only the introduction of hydrocarbon fuel that led to their falling into decay through the myth of instantaneous energy at virtually no cost. Now the cost is escalating but the old proven sustainable energy sources no longer exist.

If all the historic plants were recreated and provided with the benefits of modern turbine design and generating plant then these alone could provide a major part of the local energy consumption. It would be virtually impossible for micro plants to be centrally managed as part of a centralised main electrical grid system.

The most fundamental problems is the instantaneous nature of electricity, to the extent that the power generating companies have to produce exactly the same amount of power demanded by their consumers. This is not on a day to day, or even hour to hour basis, but on a part second to part second basis. The reality is, that if the consumer turns on an electric heater, that power has to instantaneously supplied by the grid and somewhere in the system the additional power has to be generated at the same instant in time.

In the case of a large nuclear plant, it takes several days to bring these plants up to the full operating temperature. Changes in output can only be achieved gradually, with the result that, once the generating companies have these enormous plants operating, they are very loathe to slow or shut them down.

Equally with many thousands of small plants the problems of matching overall power consumption with every individual micro generator becomes an impossible control situation.

It is impossible to store electricity in any substantial quantity even for a few seconds. Therefore, a generating company is being forced to construct both their generating plant and their transmission network to meet the peak maximum demand, despite the fact that for the majority of the time it is only being partially utilised. Equally they utilise the smaller generating plant and those with a very quick start up time to balance the loads with the result that many of the zero & low pollution plants are turned off frequently simply wasting free available energy.

There has to be put in place an energy management system that automatically stores all surplus energy from each individual plant rather than constantly trying to shut down power generation to balance the supply and demand cycles. It has to be ridiculous to turn off wind turbines, and pay the operating companies to not generate power, simply because instantaneous demand is lowered.

The tidal flows around ocean coastlines is one other potential energy source available that is not directly dependent on the sun's energy. These tidal streams are primarily caused by the relative motion of the moon and to a lesser extent the sun. It would be impractical to construct tidal generators for individual power because of the legalities of whether a tidal generator on the seabed could be operated. This does not detract from the real possibility of installing free flow tidal stream generators along coastlines with significant tidal energy. These would need to supply local communities in the first instance with any surplus power diverted to hydrogen production.

The technology already exists and trial generators have been commissioned that demonstrate the feasibility of tapping this resource. SMD Hydrovision* have developed and tested a relatively low power tidal generator which could be put into manufacture and installed around the country. As usual the problem is that due to the cyclic nature of the tides these generators do not produce power consistently to meet demand with the result that they are considered uneconomic, as a major part of the potential power would be unused with the current distribution system.

Solar energy also creates the winds, waves and currents and approximately 400 TW of the sun's energy is absorbed. It has been estimated that up to 10TW could be recoverable through wind turbines. The wind farm is now a common sight around exposed ridges and headlands, with each turbine rated typically at around 500 kW with the added eyesore of more pylons to carry away the power. Historically, wind power has been used for energy to run machinery or pump water throughout Europe for centuries. The size and scale of modern wind farms is sometimes criticised, however these machines do produce truly sustainable energy.

This technology is well understood and developed with proposed new offshore wind farms that can provide a substantial increase in rated power availability. In order to avoid the ridiculous situation where the operators are paid to not produce power these large turbine towers are obvious storage tanks for compressed hydrogen which can be made from the unused power.

Again micro wind generators are also a viable and technically available option in any area where there is significant and reasonably consistent wind. It is understood that horizontal axis turbines are suited to wind farms where turbines are aligned to the steady wind direction and these make a significant contribution to overall supply. However a vertical axis machines are better in situations where the wind direction is variable and inconsistent and these can make a useful contribution in many situations.

Direct sunlight arrives at the earth's surface at an average of 1 kW per m^2 during the hours of daylight. In practical terms, the incident solar energy on a south facing roof of 50 m^2 is 350kWh per day, assuming seven hours of sunlight. Even with a collection efficiency of 10% this would provide 35KWh per day, sufficient power for an efficient household averaged over the full year.

One of the problems with solar panels is that their efficiency drops as the temperature of the panel rises. It is a relatively simple matter to fit thermal cooling to the underside of the panels which not only increases the efficiency of the electrical power generated but also provides a ready source of thermal energy which can be utilised both for domestic hot water and building heating systems. The collection of this extra energy certainly provides a substantial benefit below latitude 40 deg and in these latitudes can increase the energy collected by over 50%.

Herein lies the fundamental problem with solar sources because the energy is not available when the demand is high and it certainly not consistent throughout the year. Electricity is the cleanest and most efficient form of energy, however it is impractical to store even for relatively short periods. The reality is that we have proved and tried technology for generating power from truly renewable resources, but we cannot control nature to have this power available at both the time and place required by demand.

One of the main attractions of a hydrogen based energy system is that micro plants become viable, enabling significant increases in power generation capacity without the environmental impact of major generating plants. This opens the option for all rural areas to return to self-sufficiency and even major cities, providing a significant part of their energy use.

It seems inconceivable that virtually no investment or research has been channelled into solving this problem. In 1839, Sir William Grove demonstrated a reversible gas cell. His experiment consisted of a pair of platinum black electrodes sealed into two-inverted glass test tubes, partially immersed in an electrolyte of dilute sulphuric acid. If a voltage is applied across the terminals then gas is given off and held in the inverted tubes. Hydrogen is given off at the cathode, negative, and oxygen at the anode, positive. The process is energy efficient and the energy stored in the hydrogen gas provides a transportable and versatile fuel, very similar to hydrocarbon gases but with none of the pollution. However if a load is connected across the terminals then the cell produces electrical power until the gases are used up.

The fundamental difference is that when generating power, or on combustion, the only product is water, identical in quantity and chemical composition to the water used to provide the hydrogen in the first instance. The process is sustainable and renewable with no pollution. It is important to note that the electrolyte, in this case dilute sulphuric acid, remains unchanged throughout the whole process. If the cell is only used for hydrogen production, the concentration of the electrolyte will steadily increase and will need periodic dilution by the addition of pure water only.

In practice, an alternative electrolyte is sodium chloride, more commonly known as salt. Seawater could be used as the electrolyte and as the end product is pure water, not only would the system provide a pollution free cycle but also the by-product would be drinking water. Considerable research would be needed to create an efficient cell that would operate continuously using seawater as the electrolyte, because all the other chemicals and organisms present in the marine environment would tend to build up within the cell.

If the world energy system were to be miraculously converted to hydrogen, would another environmental disaster lie unseen round the corner? It is essential that the overall effect on the planet and the whole ecosystem should be considered in order to ensure that the natural balance is maintained.

The basic pollution equation is balanced as the only by-product is pure water, which would be immediately returned to the environment either in the form of a vapour or simply as liquid water. This eliminates the greenhouse gas problem but also removes the fumes and hidden pollutants from the atmosphere that we, and the trees, breathe. The benefit of this alone should pressurise governments to at least encourage production and development.

On the assumption that the current world energy demand is 13 Tw continuous energy use, then we would have to provide a one months world energy storage to ensure that there was always sufficient energy available to meet demand. Even at the extreme we need to store 7,200 Twh and this is the equivalent of eight thousand million kg of water converted to hydrogen gas, a reduction in sea level of less than 1mm, or smaller than the change in sea level currently being seen every year as we continue to burn hydrocarbon fuel. The difference with the hydrogen system is that this would be a one-off event and after the initial storage is in place, there is no further change.

Hydrogen provides a perfect medium for storing energy, which can be converted back to useable power on demand. It is more economic to transport the hydrogen through pipelines than transfer power via the main electric grid systems. In practice, if a major trunk grid system of hydrogen filled gas pipelines were to replace the existing national electric grid, these would themselves provide a vast store of hydrogen to meet the fluctuations in demand. This advantage alone would make it a practical proposition to convert our electrical and distance energy transmission system to a hydrogen based system, with localised generators for each community. The conversion would be gradual so changes can be phased with the eventual balance between major generating plants and localised production.

The gas can be used in any gas burning appliance: central heating boilers, cookers etc, with only minor changes to the gas jet size to give maximum efficiency. It must be remembered that Town Gas as supplied to most cities up to the sixties, was mainly hydrogen and the conversion would simply be a reversal of the modifications made then to change over to hydrocarbon gas.

Hydrogen can be used as a fuel for most engines, with

modifications to the fuel delivery system, but all engines will run on a duel fuel mixture with the original fuel supplied at tick over speed and the hydrogen used for further increases in power and speed. In reality any engine converted to run on LPG (liquid petroleum gas) can be simply modified to run just on hydrogen. There is no reason why the hydrocarbon fuel currently used for transport could not be cut by at least 80% in the short term, at minimal change over cost, by the introduction of duel fuel running. It only requires the availability of hydrogen gas in sufficient volume and the motivation to make the change. The use in this way will not eliminate pollution entirely or result in overall improvements in efficiency but does offer a pathway to conversion.

The major car manufacturers have significantly improved the efficiency of cars over the last few decades but although the improvements have been dramatic, the efficiency is still under 40%. Considerable research is underway on alternative car propulsion, but most of this is not being channelled into the use of hydrogen as the primary energy source. The reason is a combination of financial and political pressure from themselves, due to heavy past investment in engine research from the oil and energy industry who promote their current products and from governments who would like to see a clean environment in principle, but will not take the lead or the risk of a major change in the energy balance.

Hydrogen is ideally suited for use in gas turbines and although these do not exist at present, in general use the technology is well understood and turbines could be manufactured to operate on hydrogen very quickly. The main advantage of turbines is that the overall efficiency is much higher and they are ideally suited to electricity generation.

The efficiency of a system is the useable output power as a percentage of the input power. A typical car engine runs at around 40% whereas an electric motor achieves over 90%, with the gas turbines operating at better than 50%. The current major coal or oil fired electrical generation plants achieve overall efficiencies of under 40% . Thus a modern plant producing 1,200 Mw requires a fuel input of 3,400 Mw with the loss escaping into the environment as heat. There is a further loss between the generating plant and the consumer in the electrical grid system, with this loss proportional to the physical distance between the two. Ideally the power generating plants should be situated inside major cities and industrial areas to keep the transmission losses to a minimum.

In the summer of 2003, the eastern seaboard of the USA and Canada suffered a major blackout lasting several days due to the failure of the grid system, while London and Italy had a power cuts for a few hours. These were the result of massive amounts of power being transmitted over long distances through a grid network that requires modernisation and upgrading. The grid systems were built when energy was cheap and power stations were moved away from major population centres to hide the pollution. Now with the cost of energy increasing, the funds are not available to maintain and upgrade any of the infrastructure resulting in the failures now commonly seen in all the major service providers. It is not coincidental that the rail networks were built in the heyday of the coal industry and the roads when cheap oil was flowing freely. The maintenance of this infrastructure has fallen on a time when energy costs are rising, resulting in resources being pinched.

Hydrogen power generation plants could be located within urban and industrial areas simply because they are totally non-polluting. If electrical power generation evolved into small, localised generating stations there would be two major advantages. Firstly, the waste heat could be readily provided to the local area for domestic heating, effectively reducing overall energy use. Secondly, the transmission loss would virtually disappear, dramatically improving the overall efficiency and removing dependence on the integrity of the overall grid system.

The fuel cell has existed for over fifty years and simply reverses the electrolysis reaction that produces the hydrogen in the first place. The fuel cell's efficiency is in excess of 80% and the output is electricity. Currently these are relatively expensive but mass usage would quickly bring the costs down to economic levels and in one simple stroke, the world energy consumption could be reduced by almost 50%. It is important to understand that at present, we waste well over half of the total energy consumed, in waste heat, let loose into our rivers and atmosphere. Changing over to a hydrogen and fuel cell based energy system would increase the overall efficiency to around 70%, after allowing for the energy loss in the hydrogen production and the subsequent conversion back into electricity when needed.

For every kWh of fossil fuel consumed providing electrical

power to the consumer, over half a kW is wasted at the point of generation and the further 10% is then used up getting this generated electricity to the consumer. The end result is that for every 1 kWh of fossil fuel supplied to generating stations only 0.4 kWh actually arrived at the consumer. The moment we introduce a system where a generation is localised, any surplus thermal energy can be consumed by the consumer therefore improving the overall energy efficiency of the whole system.

This is the political nightmare, as each individual or household could produce hydrogen, store it and subsequently utilise it for cooking, heating and their own private electrical requirements. It would prove difficult, if not impossible, to quantify the energy both produced and used. The government revenues depend significantly on taxes of all fuels and energy consumption, and if this is returned to the individual, then the present system could fail. In political terms, a society where energy production was in the domain of each individual is unthinkable to the current centralised governments, as real independence of the individual would undoubtedly cause major changes in the current political structure.

At present, if a smallholder has a few trees growing, so that over a ten or fifteen year cycle they produce sufficient firewood to meet the household heating needs, then this wood is tax free. His trees are absorbing the sun's energy and through photosynthesis, growing wood to provide domestic heating. This is a traditional right in all society and up to the mid nineteenth century, was the primary energy source. The reality is that the agricultural and rural environment provided not only their own wood for domestic fuel, but also supplied the cities and urban areas, providing a significant cash crop to the producers. There is no difference whether the incoming sun's energy is used to grow wood on agricultural land, or turn a wind turbine or fall directly on a solar panel and the conversion of this to hydrogen is simply a means of storing surplus energy in a readily useable form.

The hydrogen is produced from the sun's energy falling on his property, in the same way as his trees grow, and he uses it for heating and cooking. He might also chose to run his car and provide the household with electrical power making himself independent of the power and energy companies. This is the point at which the lack of political will to encourage and promote small-scale energy production suddenly makes sense.

The existing major energy providers will certainly discourage any development along these lines, as it would quickly erode their own market share as well as completely changing the power balance. At present we have a handful of major energy providers, supplying both business and the private individual as virtual monopolies. The recent moves to privatise the energy suppliers has simply moved existing major generating plants and distribution networks to different names. The reality is that there is no real choice for the individual as all the different deals still send the power down the same cables or pipes to each user from the same generating plants.

The governments are currently beginning the conditioning process for the construction of major new nuclear plants, on the basis that these provide a sustainable energy supply that does not create greenhouse gas emissions and thus environmentally friendly. This statement is fundamentally true, but the economics can only be justified if you simply ignore the cost of decommissioning the plant and can only be justified if you are prepared to take the ostrich approach and simply pretend that the decommission is not a problem. As for the risk, this can be dismissed on the basis that the new plants will be better designed and that improvements in technology have made nuclear energy very safe, which is fine if you are prepared to ignore the constant string of significant nuclear escapes and incidents that have happened consistently, since nuclear power was first introduced and totally discount medical evidence that indicates that incidents of diseases, actually cancers, increases with the proximity to nuclear plants. If there really was an overall shortage of energy, then the promotion of nuclear plants would make some sort of sense, but when there is a perfectly viable and totally safe alternative, promotion by the government and the energy providers must be seriously questioned.

The oil companies will also discourage any major shift to hydrogen, as their core business is the extraction, refining and sale of hydrocarbon fuel. Any significant move to use hydrogen, as a major fuel source, will immediately cut their sales and profits from oil, especially if produced locally for each community. They are also the only winners while the oil price heads skyward, reaping windfall profits every year due to the escalation in price.

The natural simplicity of hydrogen production lends itself to small scale production but conversely, the problems encountered in major production plants are quite difficult to resolve. In essence, an electrolysis cell for the production of hydrogen is very similar to a large car battery, but with power constantly fed into the cell. The power is consumed at approximately 1.5 to 2.4 volts in each individual cell and a small scale bank of cells would comprise 3 or 8 individual cells in series. Thus to make hydrogen, the input voltage needs to be very low, 6 volts for a series bank of 4 cells and 12 volts for a series bank of 6 cells.

The converse to this low voltage is that the current in amps is high, so for a 1kW hydrogen generator the input current at 12 volts would be 83 amps continuously. This is comparable to the starting current for a lorry with a normal battery, but continuously. The size of the electrical cable necessary to carry this current needs to be 10mm and even then the cable will become warm in use. The energy loss in the transmission cables is proportional to the square of the current, in other words, if the current doubles then the power loss is increased by a factor of four.

Imagine the complications of converting a 5Mw wind turbine to hydrogen production. If this was carried out in a 12 volt electrolysis cell, the input current would be 83,000 amps requiring a cable several meters in diameter. If a hundred cells were used in parallel then the current would be reduced to 830 amps, but still needing massive cables and connections and every extra centimetre of cable further increases the power loss. This is still a practical possibility but would need careful design and development and would by its nature need a major capital investment and time to install and operate. These are the problems currently being tackled in Iceland, where large geothermal plants are converting surplus energy to hydrogen production.

If industrial size conversion plants are utilised to produce hydrogen then the overall efficiency will invariably be compromised so this is where we should learn from nature. Every tree has multiple conversion cells in every leaf and thousands of leaves overall so despite the minimal energy transfer in each individual cell the total energy transferred is substantial.

It possible to create hydrogen using an electric arc which would separate the oxygen and the hydrogen into gaseous form. These gases then have to be separated by heating: they are an explosive combination. This technology does provide an alternative method of utilising electricity generated at both high voltages and in high power outputs, but the overall efficiency is lower and the plant has to be exceptionally carefully managed to ensure there is no risk of explosion.

At this power level the initial investment would be higher but it would enable all the potential power to be collected from all renewable resources, most significantly wind, tidal and hydro. At present the renewable generating plant already in place is not fully utilised because the power generated is not always available to meet the instantaneous demand, so the massive nuclear or fuel burning generating plants are always running, simply because they cannot just be switched on and off at will. It takes many hours, sometimes days, to get these plants up to full running temperature and once up and running, the generating boards have to keep them operating continuously. Therefore the wind turbines and the hydro stations are turned off until needed and always play second fiddle to the massive thermal plants.

A fundamental shift to small localised electric generating plants would ensure that every plant had a short start up period, measured in minutes, so that any changes in demand could be covered immediately. This would save the energy loss in transmitting the power over long distances as well as ensuring that no plants are kept ticking over just to prevent them cooling down. Contrary to the current system, the existing renewable generators would always be running at maximum capacity with the gas powered plants only in use to supply peaks in demand.

Converting the output from a small wind turbine rated at 1kW to hydrogen is a straightforward process. All the equipment is currently manufactured and available commercially and the unit cost is approximately 0.056 Euro per kWh. This is directly comparable with existing prices and of course, once the system is installed, the unit cost will remain static against the general trend of rising energy prices. The majority of the cost of the individual system is the finance of the capital originally invested, which traditionally in the power business is calculated over a ten year period.

This makes financial sense when considering mechanical plant, like rotating generators, which will require replacement periodically, but is onerously restrictive when applied to renewable resources.

Based on these criteria, it is a fact that most hydroelectric systems are considered unviable when the project is started, due to the high capital investment in dams, high pressure feed pipes and the invariable long connection to the existing grid system. However once the initial ten year period has expired, with all the initial capital investment repaid with interest, then the hydro system continues to function without any further major investment and produces virtually free electricity. It must be nonsensical to apply criteria that completely ignore this long-term reality, whether this is continual free electricity with the best of the renewable systems or the prohibitive cost of decommissioning associated with nuclear plants. The current energy producers set these criteria so it is hardly surprising that they appear to justify the status quo.

As far as individuals are concerned, the criteria must surely be whether power can be generated at a competitive cost, allowing for realistic financing of the original capital investment over the expected life of each part of the system. If these criteria were used then solar panels and hydrogen cells would have an expected life of at least 50 years whereas the life for wind turbines would be 7 to 15 years. However the infrastructure investment is still long term so the replacement cost of wind turbines only relates to the actual mechanical generating unit not the tower or other infrastructure.

Equally, capturing the sun's energy directly in photovoltaic cells and storing any surplus energy in hydrogen can utilise the same hydrogen cell as a wind turbine. It is thus realistically feasible today for any householder to purchase, install and operate a hydrogen energy system.

Essentially, all forms of energy derived from variable renewable sources must have the capability of storing their surplus energy production for future use. Unless this is an integral part of any project, then the viability will always be doubtful, simply because the project will be under utilised from the outset. Whether this takes the form of simply switching off the generators at times of low demand, or an economic adjustment of the value of the generated power, is academic.

The feasibility of the introduction of hydrogen as an alternative energy source is both technically practical and financially realistic, both on an individual basis and as part of the existing renewable energy infrastructure. There is always a resistance to any change, in this case amplified by the interests of the existing energy giants, although historically any new industry promotes a massive burst of new infrastructure building, bringing with it employment and real growth. The pessimists will advocate a collapse of the system, with tax revenues falling and society unable to maintain the welfare services. However, the reality must be that if real wealth is created, then the distribution is a matter of choice and at the present time, we are unable to balance the economies and have no options.

Even setting aside both nuclear and geo-thermal power generation both of which produce power without atmospheric pollution there is ample opportunity to meet energy needs by installation of solar, wind, hydro and tidal generating plants. These generating options have to be considered on the micro level rather than trying to consolidate these into the historic centralised systems.

Chapter 5
Consumption

The initial concept of this book started in the spring of 2001 and evolved during that summer, resulting in serious research into an individual sustainable energy system. This was before Mr. Bush had publicly committed himself to dealing with Saddam Hussein and maintaining that oil would stay below the 30$ barrel level.

From 2004, with the crude oil price fluctuating around 45$ a barrel, even in the UK with its overall self sufficiency, the cost of delivered crude oil to the refineries determines the current high energy price, but with the cost of extraction and delivery leaving little margin of profit. The real wealth generated is thus a small part of the total energy cost and this is the fundamental reason why the developed world is struggling to balance their economies. The energy that used to gush from low cost wells is now history. Instead, we have complex wellheads in hostile environments with extended delivery systems. Nature is no longer allowing us to pillage her reserves, and now they have to be extracted at high cost.

This energy price filters its way through the system adding to both manufacturing costs and each individual's overheads, creating the spiral of higher wages further pressurising prices. The French economy is a particularly good example, partly because there are no major national oil reserves, leading to an

French Primary Energy & Consumption MTOE (2003)

	Coal	Oil	Gas	Nuclear	Hydro	Renewables	Total
National production **	1.5	1.9	1.5	110	6.8	11.9	133.6
Energy Imports **	10.3	93.9	35.0	-5.9	0	0	133.3
Total Primary Energy **	11.8	95.8	36.5	104.1	6.8	11.9	266.9
% of Total of Primary Energy	4.5	35.8	13.7	39.0	2.5	4.5	100
French Consumption **	6.6	75.6	31.2	34.4	10.7		158.5
Energy Lost in Transport & Generation to Consumer	5.2	20.2	5.3	70.6	10.1		102.5
% loss in relation to Total Primary Energy	44	21	14	67	10		33

Source Observatoire de l'energie **
Consumption Figures for electricity combine both Nuclear & Hydroelectric

Energy loss for Hydrocarbon fuels only allows for refining costs (5 MTOE) and electrical consumption within this sector (4 Mtoe)
The majority of the loss in Coal relates to electricity production (11 used to produce 4 Mtoe Electricity)

early interest and development of renewable resources, as France is also representative of modern society in the developed world, far from the extreme of the USA, but a good balance within Europe.

France's primary energy use for a population of 56 million totals 266.9 Mtoe (2003), with the total hydrocarbon fuel imports at 95.8 Mtoe in oil and 36.5 Mtoe in gas, representing just under 50%. The net effect on the balance of payments, at 26$ barrel, amounts to 24.5 billion Euros, which is substantially higher than the government deficit in 2002 of 21 billion Euros.

Even if the primary energy use in 2004 does not increase, then this figure would rise to approximately 32 billion Euros at the current oil price (calculated at 37$ a barrel). It is not coincidental that the deficit has risen to an estimated 35 billion Euros in 2003, which is directly comparable to the actual cost to the economy due to the rising level of oil prices in the same period.

It is an inescapable fact that this has to be paid from the wealth created within the French economy and that these funds leave France. They are not available within the country for investment in the infrastructure or to meet the government's current account liabilities. If the wealth were retained within France, then as an absolute minimum this vast sum would be available within the economy.

It is equally arguable that the effect would, in reality, be several times greater, as funds revolve within the economy creating additional employment, with increased tax revenues. It is a well established economic theory that investment in infrastructure to create employment, thereby reducing unemployment benefits, whilst at the same time increasing tax income, is a way of boosting an economy. The flaw is that governments cannot pursue these policies based solely on increased government borrowing because the debt quickly spirals out of control. The situation is completely different if the investment stems from genuine wealth creation within the system.

A report in the summer of 2004 by eminent world economists concluded that the French economy was stagnating, with the government facing ongoing problems with both the budget deficit and the balance of payments. These factors would result in steadily increasing unemployment with the treasury struggling to meet commitments for both unemployment benefits and pensions. Major changes in public sector spending would be required in order to reduce the burden on the exchequer. In simplistic terms, the government will not be able to pay the pensions in full or maintain the social services at the present level. A simple conclusion for an economist sitting in their ivory tower, but a disaster for those who have paid into the welfare system all their working lives; anticipating a secure and comfortable retirement.

It is not that the specialists have come to the wrong conclusion; they have projected forward the current financial models to provide an insight into the future. Within the parameters of these models the conclusions are undoubtedly realistic and justifiable. The problem is that the model is fundamentally flawed, because if hydrocarbon fuel remains the main energy source then the price will undoubtedly escalate well above inflation. The economic projections would then be completely thrown out because the basic parameters used in their economic model are changed for the worse.

If the price of crude starting in January 2005 at 45$ with inflationary increases for the next ten years at 2.5%, then the final price in 2015 would be 59.04$, whereas if the price is also escalated by a shortage factor of only 10% pa then the final price is 164.45 $. The effect on the balance of payments is that the French economy would have to pay 142 billion Euros annually for fuel oil which could only result in the collapse of the system.

In fact the financial crisis in 2008 stopped the steady increase in oil prices and created a few more years off apparent stability but all indication are that these will now climb again.

Thus if you follow the officially perceived trends, then the results generated by the models will drastically understate the decline in the market. However if you reversed this by utilising capital investment to create a renewable energy regime, then not only would there be no loss of wealth within the economy but the additional activity would mitigate the current account deficit.

Economists argue that the current level of energy prices are containable and will not affect the stability of the economy. The reasoning is that energy costs represent a small part of each process and thus do not have a significant overall effect on the economy as a whole.

This assumption must be fundamentally flawed because, at the end of the day, all our products are created from the raw materials available on the planet. These we do not have to create because they are a free bonus, whether they be metallic deposits or any other raw material that we can utilise in order to provide goods for the consumer.

It is the conversion of the raw materials into the form needed that starts the process towards the consumer. Invariably this conversion is energy expensive and a substantial part of the added value is due to the energy input. Even the workforce employed to create the product requires energy to exist and work, amounting to 2 kWh in food energy per day, let alone the energy consumed in their personal domestic situation. It is more realistic to consider virtually the whole of the added value is related to the energy utilised in the conversion of the raw materials to a viable product.

Iron and steel have been integral to human development, and the manufacturing process is straightforward in principle. The first step is to find and collect a high yielding iron ore and this is one of the most common elements and is readily available.

The iron ore needs to be mixed with limestone and carbon, originally in the form of charcoal, and all these lie in the ground or are available from the surrounding forest. This mixture is then heated in a furnace with the result that the iron will be isolated from the ore and will settle to the bottom of the furnace with slag above. Once the whole process is completed and allowed to cool the iron can be broken out from the furnace. The product is a basic form of cast iron but repeated heating in a charcoal forge, and hammering to remove residual impurities, can further work the ingot.

The final product is wrought iron, which has similar properties to mild steel. This formed the basis of all iron products for many centuries, until specialised steels were developed at the end of the nineteenth century.

One man could complete this task where the three basic ingredients were available and it should take between 10 to 15 days to produce around one kilogram of iron. The energy calculation is thus simple:
One man for 15 days @ 2 kWh pd == 30 kWh
1 Kg Charcoal   == 0.75 kWh.

If allowance is made for transport to the nearest town, the total cost of the produced iron amounts to approximately 33 kWh. per Kg of iron which can now be turned into a Roman sword or plough blade. All the input energy is derived from the sun, both to provide food for the man and the wood for the charcoal.

The fundamental question is whether the monetary value of the produce is quantifiably related to the production energy consumption.

Money evolved as a means of simplifying the exchange of goods, enabling the whole available range to be assessed on a common scale. Otherwise it would have been necessary for the iron maker to swap lumps of iron for food, clothing and any other items required by his family unit.

The question is whether the value allocated to any particular product related directly to the quantity of energy utilised in its creation. This is true in a subsistence economy, where foodstuffs are the primary source of wealth and barter of goods is more relevant than any numerical value arbitrarily allocated to any particular product. The situation becomes confused as society evolves and non-essential products enter the market, but it is still realistic to relate the total energy cost of any product to its value.

In practice, considerable experience is needed both to select the ore and the proportions of the materials. The result is that individuals specialised in iron production but needed to provide for both themselves and their families. In effect their energy requirements escalated as the whole family needed food, clothing and housing and the value of the iron rose to between 50 and 100 kWh per Kg.

The successful iron makers built water mills to power bellows and power driven hammers to improve both the quantity and quality of their production. In effect, they utilised a part of their created wealth to construct the mill and extracted additional hydraulic power from the rivers and streams to improve their production. Despite the fact that this additional energy was from fully sustainable sources, at the end of the day, the cost in energy terms of a kilogram of iron at best remained the same but most probably increased due to the inefficiencies within the mill. This was offset by better quality and a more consistent product, therefore it is realistic to envisage a price adjustment that still reflected the real input energy costs.

The investment in man hours to construct the mill can be assessed in energy terms, which is subsequently repaid by improved production in the future.

The reality is that if mechanical plant replaces manual labour, there appears to be an energy saving. However, the truth is that this is more than offset by the fuel costs of operating the plant and the hidden manufacturing energy cost in the fabricating of the plant initially. In essence everything created by a manufacturing process could be measured simply in energy terms. A mechanical excavator is created from steel, machined and cast specifically for the final product and the cost can be expressed as the cumulative value of the input energy. Equally, as this equipment is used, this then can be considered as a depreciation of the energy encapsulated within the machinery.

It is not unreasonable to assume that the whole of the added value for any product can be related to energy with the sole exception of the manufacturer's net profit from the operation. As the latter is in the order of 10% it could be argued that 90% of all products are energy dependent.

So with all items there are two types of energy involved. The most straightforward is the direct energy used in the process and the subsequent transport. The human energy of the employees should also be included in this assessment, as they are integral part of the process and their energy needs must also be provided in the form of their direct energy consumption, both in food and consumed energy. The second form is the encapsulated energy in the fabric of the work environment, whether this is the steel and manufactured parts of a mechanical excavator or lorry, or simply the cost in energy terms of building the work place.

This reasoning fundamentally overturns current economic thinking. Energy is the driving force with true growth only possible with a managed and adequate available energy source. It has to be ridiculous to dismiss energy costs as a minor part of modern society, when we live in a world that literally stops in its tracks even with a short term power cut. The effect of a significant interruption in crude oil supplies would result in no transportation or electricity within days, bringing the whole system to a halt.

The linking of a society's ability to provide for its own energy needs, both in terms of sufficient food and directly consumable energy, and the success of that society, is difficult to prove clearly. Historical records do show that ancient civilisations flourished when food and energy were readily available, and that collapsing empires are synonymous with shortages. Whether it is justified to state that the downfalls were due to the shortages is another matter, but they run together.

It is clear that current levels of consumption are straining the system and even in Europe, we can only satisfy this demand by massive imports.

France Consumption 2001 (Mtoe)

Sector	Coal	Oil	Gas	Electricity	Renewable	Total
Industry	6	7.2	11.3	12	1.8	33.3
Domestic	0.6	16.8	19.6	21.3	8.5	66.8
Agriculture	0	2.4	0.3	0.2	0.1	3
Transport	0	49.2	0	0.9	0.3	50.4
Total	6.6	75.6	31.2	34.4	10.7	158.5
%	4%	47%	20%	22%	7%	

Source Observatoire de l'energie
Renewables include Wind & Hydro

It is interesting to note that the consumption of private cars is estimated at approximately 55% of the petroleum transport category, based on mileage figures with weighting for relative consumption. If this is added to the domestic usage, all the individual consumers are directly responsible for 59% of the total energy consumption. This demonstrates that fundamental issue is direct consumption by individuals. The chart below shows energy use graphically but never forget that the other sectors also exist only for the consumer. The simple and indisputable fact is that individuals consume 59% of the total energy utilised directly in their personal lives. In addition they consume more energy directly at work and at play, accounting for a further significant part of the 24% utilised in the industry and the 15% left in transport.

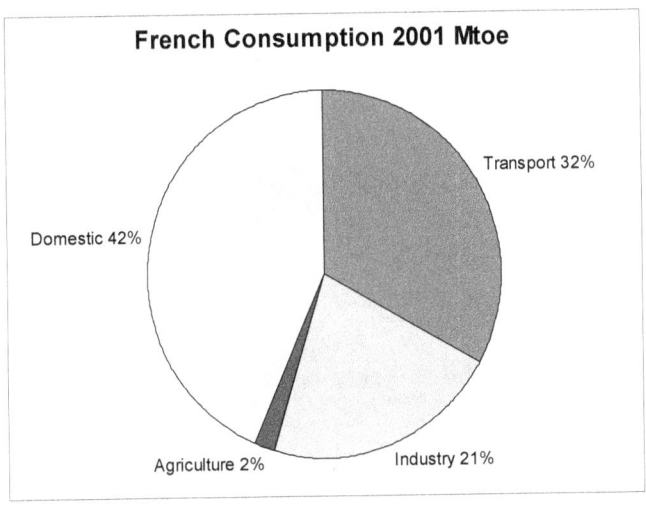

French Consumption 2001 Mtoe

Transport 32%

Domestic 42%

Agriculture 2%   Industry 21%

In France, nuclear power accounts for 77% of the total electrical production, with 5.5% equivalent to 5.9 Mtoe exported, whereas classic thermal stations only provide around 9% with the renewable's providing 14%. Due to this reliance, hydrocarbon fuel is significantly lower here than in any other state within the EU. The UK had in 1992, 18% nuclear, 8% hydro & other renewable's, with the balance being 74% hydrocarbon burning generating plant using 57.5 Mtoe.

Energy consumption is simply not something else to be dealt

with by politicians and bureaucrats. It is something that stems from the individual behaviour of every single person living on the planet and as such, must be their individual responsibility.

I listened the other day to an interview by a sceptic, albeit, he was representing one of the major oil companies, who simply stated that even if every single car in the United Kingdom was garaged immediately, and all private transport ceased, the benefit to the planet's ecosystem would be back to its current level within a year, simply due to the growth of consumption. Whether this statement is actually factually true or not, is probably questionable, but the statement does appear to reflect the substance of the figures for private car usage within the United Kingdom and the projected growth of the Chinese economy.

The more frightening part is the ostrich approach, reflected in his attitude, suggesting that the total UK car consumption was small compared with world global consumption, that it is simply not worth dealing with and that somehow the system will be put right at some stage in the future.

This is the Titanic approach in solving a problem, where a proposal is put forward that the ships company should have bailed out with a teacup. This clearly would have had very little effect, so the idea evolved and consideration is given to every single passenger bailing out of the Titanic with a teacup, and even extended to providing them with buckets, which of course results in massive amounts of calculations and estimates of the quantity of water that can be thrown overboard by a man who will drown if he does not succeed.

Depending on the calculations and ignoring whether these calculations are actually feasibly practical, it is quite possible to have a long and extended discussion over their viability. The real answer is undoubtedly that one man could cut the power on the engines and the boat would slow down, and when moving slowly, the course could be changed to a southerly course, thereby completely avoiding the collision with the iceberg. This completely eliminates the argument over teacups, and with hindsight, every single passenger and crew would agree that it was the correct decision.

All the developed economies are stagnating and the exponential growth in the pacific economies is being fuelled by very low energy use per person within their populations, thus enabling them to supply manufactured goods to the developed economies cheaper than those economies can produce themselves.

As their energy costs per individual climb, they will lose their competitive edge. The problem is quite simply that if the less developed nations in the world increase their personal energy consumption, to anything like that of even Europe, then there is no possibility of that energy being provided from known reserves. It is essential that world consumption of fossil fuel is dramatically slowed down and replaced by a truly sustainable energy regime. This is because it is the individuals who consume the bulk of the energy, therefore it is a problem that has to solved by the individuals and it simply cannot be resolved by governments alone.

Chapter 6
Agriculture

The agricultural conundrum is that farm subsidies in one form or another make agriculture in the developed world an industry that simply manages to stagger from one year to the next. The farmers are not generating substantial financial surpluses, resulting in limited reinvestment, with the younger generations looking for simpler and more certain employment.

Historically this was certainly not always the case; just consider the substantial estates built across Europe in previous centuries. These vast properties were essentially constructed from the wealth generated from the agricultural operations without the necessity for government subsidies, and this would be utterly impossible with the current profitability in farming. There are well documented properties built with funds totally independent of agriculture but in the main, most estates were built from wealth derived from the lands.

As an example, a single domain in France, built around two hundred years ago comprises a main house of 200m2, a manager's house of 160m2, workers cottages of 180m2 and two stone barns on two floors of 800m2. At current building prices the construction cost of the residential property would be approximately 800,000 Euros with a further similar sum for the construction of the barns. The total building cost for this property at today's prices would be over 1.6 million Euros (£1,400,000) and this was clearly considered a realistic investment for a property operating only 40 Ha of land and vineyards.

Clearly these figures reflect the current building costs but those at the time were consistent with the time of the investment. However, the reality is that although inflation has made the numerical values higher, at least over the last century, building costs have remained essentially static in real terms.

The older building methods were more labour intensive but a traditional stone built property with hand hewn timber beams would certainly be more expensive to construct today. The fact that a substantial part of the labour force was undoubtedly the on-site farm workers, using slack times on the farm to make capital improvements to the properties, does not detract from the wealth created by the construction work. These old structures have stood the test of time and I doubt if many buildings constructed today with 10cm load bearing walls will still be standing a couple of centuries in the future. Modern services have obviously added to current building costs but overall the comparison is realistic even if not exactly correct.

The inflation table in chapter 1 demonstrates that prices in real terms have remained static or similar over an extended time period. It is also true that the source data is not consistent throughout the whole period in that the accommodation and facilities provided within a low cost housing unit have significantly varied. In 1850 a good property was expected to have one external toilet and cold running water to the kitchen area with no other connected services. Progress by 1975 had conditioned occupiers to expect all services connected, internal bathroom with hot and cold running water and as such a direct comparison of housing costs ignores these enhancements.

The fact that cereal (bread) costs are by far the lowest, reflect the subsidies applied specifically to lower the cost of basic foodstuffs. In effect, the agricultural enterprises are now paid less than a third of the historic price in real terms for their produce and left totally dependent on subsidies to provide even a basic income. These subsidies are funded from the taxes, which have been introduced over the last century, and effectively cut income thus making the foodstuffs a dramatically higher proportion of net income. The subsidy on beef has been far less consistent and at a much lower rate than is reflected in the apparent premium cost of beef today.

So today this same land will produce an income of a maximum 10,000 Euros/pa, before taxes, of which at least 5,000 Euros is farm subsidy. The reality is that the farmer will be lucky to earn the equivalent of a normal salary with virtually no net disposable income; there is certainly no prospect of embarking on a major investment programme sufficient to construct this type of property.

Originally the farm would have operated with working livestock, with almost certainly a few additional animals for food and to provide additional cash income. There would have been at least 10Ha set aside for animal grazing or fodder, and most probably a further 5Ha for cash crops of such as cereals and vegetables. The net effect was a balanced system with the animals providing, together with the pressings from the 25Ha of grapes, more than sufficient fertilizer to ensure the system was fully independent and sustainable. There would have been adequate trees on the land to provide firewood for their own heating and cooking needs, with almost certainly a further surplus providing yet another annual cash income.

In practice there was no bought in energy, all their requirements were derived from the incoming suns radiation even to the extent of the basic food to keep the whole system of families well fed. In effect the farm would have functioned viably even without the vineyards leaving the whole of the income, with the exception of the bottling costs, from the wine as clear profit. They should have produced over 100,000 bottles a year with today's prices at 4-10 Euros a bottle, which provides some insight as to why the investment originally took place. The changes are relatively recent phenomena, the use of mechanical plant and dependence of external sources of energy has both been introduced since the end of the Second World War.

The resident workforce comprised the owner together with his immediate family and the manager's family both housed in separate substantial properties. Additionally the cottages would have provided sufficient accommodation for a further family plus at least another couple. In effect there would have been at least five working men as permanent employees together with their partners and any semi adult children or grandparents.
This workforce is sufficient to manage the estate in terms of ensuring the animals and crops are properly tended.

The resident workforce could have covered all the routine maintenance, or even capital improvements to the properties and farm. The only additional labour that would have been required would have been transient labour to assist with the main harvest in September. In terms of salaries these would have been ridiculously low at first sight. In reality the whole unit is self sufficient, so the salaries paid are in addition to the basic living requirements as all housing, property fuel costs and food are already provided by the unit. In real terms the salaries paid are net disposable income.

This is an almost feudal situation not so much because of the low level of net income but because of the total dependence of all the workers on the estate on any whims or demands of the principal.

This seems initially virtually unacceptable but all the work is on site with the result that commuting time is zero. Compare this to the average worker today who may work a forty hour week but will almost certainly have between one and four hours commuting every day. The real working week, taken from leaving home to returning, is over fifty hours which begins to make even a historical six day week at eight hours a day all on the farm look attractive.

The same applies to the wages, the average family today cannot even balance the budget on a single wage let alone have a significant disposable income after all bills and living expenses have been paid. In reality, there is currently no freedom of choice as most family units are trapped in an expenditure cycle that forces the wage earners to continue working just to keep their heads above the mire. The reality is that most mothers are compelled to return to work as the second wage is necessary. The question is whether a real disposable income albeit tied into a dependent working environment is a better option than no real income after expenses but with perceived independence.

Today the same rural unit relies heavily on farm subsidies and the animals have gone, replaced by tractors of various types. Even the irrigation windmills have rusted away to be replaced by diesel or electric pumps. The workforce has been cut from three or four families down to one operating manager and the odd temporary labour. The pastureland has been replanted with vines and most of the trees have been cut down leaving the land exposed to the elements. There is no home produced fertiliser so the chemical shortages are bought in from the factories and dumped on the crops in the spring. The soil is depleted of microbes and nature's vast range of creatures has been largely killed by the regular use of pesticides so the natural regeneration processes have all but been stopped. This leaves the crop vulnerable to attack from any range of insects or fungus disease so we spray again with more pesticide and fungicide, just to make sure that absolutely nothing is left alive. All these chemical are expensive both in cash terms but also in terms of the energy utilised in their manufacture.

From an operating point of view the farm now needs to bring in the gasoil for the machinery (3,000 L), domestic heating oil (4,000 L), electricity for the domestic use and the farming operations (2,000 Kwh or 1800 L) and of course food, as the unit is no longer self sufficient. The approximate cost of this bought in energy is just under five thousand Euros annually with a further similar sum spent on herbicides, pesticides and fertiliser. The farmer's net income has thus been cut by at least 10,000 Euros pa in real terms. These are very conservative estimates with the reality probably over 20% higher.

The food that is now purchased at the supermarket has been processed in the same way, so a high proportion of the cost of this is energy expended by other farmers and processing plants. The annual cost of feeding a family is at least 5,500 Euros pa of which probably 50% relates to energy costs in production, processing and distribution.

The secondary effect is that the small cash crops have also disappeared further reducing income but also eliminating the diversity making the farmer absolutely dependent on the mono-crop.

Historically five families were supported and these have now moved to the major towns or cities but still needing energy, foodstuffs and housing. The cost in energy terms is 1800 L pa for each displaced person or in this case approximately 16,000 L oil pa which historically was provided by the farm unit.

So not only has the supposed modernisation in the last fifty years had the effect of increasing the farms energy use by around 9,000 L gasoil pa, but society is the looser by at least a further 16,000 L gasoil. This takes no account of any firewood previously provided to the local area by the farm during the year as a bonus cash crop.

As an isolated case this can be dismissed as unfortunate but taken overall, it demonstrates how our energy use has moved from self sufficiency to absolute dependence on external energy sources not slowly over centuries in less than 30 years since the 1950's. This change has evolved only over the last century. If every 40Ha of agricultural land became self sufficient this would significantly reduce consumption of hydrocarbon fuels. However if each 40Ha unit also provided to society, from sustainable resources, the equivalent of a further 16,000 L gas oil pa, then energy problem would virtually disappear both in terms of damage by pollution and the disastrous effect to the balance of payments of the oil purchases.

The current level of farm subsidies is a significant financial burden on the European economies with pressure from both inside the EU and externally, for these subsidies to be phased out. Under the present system this can only result in both farm production falling and food prices forced higher. Neither of these options is politically acceptable.

Significant pressure is applied to Europe by the USA both directly in relation to farm subsidies but also in relation to the restrictions placed by Europeans on American agricultural methods. These have been brought to the fore by the arguments over the introduction of GM products but also apply to fertilisers and other chemicals. American farm production is not directly subsidised in the same way, but by artificially holding fuel prices at unrealistically low levels, the American government effectively subsidises both their agriculture and industry at least as significantly as Europe.

Increasing food prices will simply result in higher inflation leading to a general increase in wages. The whole point of the subsidies was to stabilise and hold down food prices by using EU revenues. This ensures continuity of food supply at lower prices thus effectively redistributing the tax revenues equally to every member of society. If food prices rise it is the poor who will suffer.

As a fundamental principle, farm production should be maintained nationally even if the produce could be obtained on the world market at a lower cash price. It is totally irrational to purchase foodstuffs from distant continents, with all the extra transportation costs, simply because in cash terms the costs are comparable. This is more a function of unrealistically fixed exchange rates resulting in poor countries being underpaid for their produce with the result that third world wages are held down.

In one way, market forces are already encouraging a shift back to a more balanced way of food production. There is no way even the most idealistic can expect farmers to revert to horse drawn ploughs and purely manual labour, but changes are practical still using modern equipment. This is the Organic farming movement which eliminates the use of manufactured chemicals for both pest, weed control and fertilizer. The principle is simply that if the farm is well managed and the soils well fertilised with natural products then the whole farm becomes a healthy living entity. Their natural predators control the pests and other diseases are minimised by good farming practices.

The slow but steady increase in Organic farms is fuelled not by subsidies or government pressure but by the consumer. The demand for food, free from chemicals, is steadily growing. It is now very rare to find a supermarket without a substantial Organic selection whereas only a few years ago it was virtually negligible. The yield from Organic farming are lower and this raises the possibility of a reduction in overall food production but the advantages of a balanced natural ecosystem cannot be simply ignored.

The Internet generally has dramatically extended the information available. It is not that the data was previously hidden, but it required dedication to locate the relevant document. Now these same documents can be accessed from any computer and as more people find information of interest this is sent round the net for anyone searching for a related subject.

The question commonly asked now, is how were chemicals, known to be potentially dangerous to life, certified for use in an industry that literally spreads thousands of tonnes all over the food destined for human consumption. Even if only trace residues are left in the food sold, this should never have even been contemplated as the remainder, not actually eaten, is allowed to percolate through the soils into the water supplies. As the pressure from environmental groups and consumers increases governments are now beginning to phase out the most toxic and lethal but usually with a delay to allow existing stocks to be cleared.

This is not an academic discussion, the simple reality is that a cocktail of chemicals specifically designed to be toxic contaminates people in Europe. A test[1] carried out in December 2003 found that every person blood tested was contaminated, although the extent of contamination in individual cases varied from a maximum of 54 with a median number of 41 chemicals per individual. At least 13 of the same chemicals were found in every person, which included chemicals banned in Europe for the last 20 years.

How this can be justified is beyond comprehension. If the substance is causing damage to the environment and is also potentially dangerous to humans to the extent that it needs to be withdrawn from sale, then logically the existing stocks should be destroyed, not phased out over a few years.

It is one thing to support industry but to do so and risk the health of the population just demonstrates the minister's attitude making decisions in their ivory towers over serious matters of state. The problem is that industrialists have direct access to both senior politicians and ministers and they take every opportunity to promote their products. Governments are always receptive to helping industry, who at the end of the day are major employers and substantial contributors to the exchequer, resulting in the temptation to allow new products into the market place.

It appears that unless clear evidence is available that a product is dangerous then it will be permitted, even though the manufacturer carries out most of the initial testing. The situation should be reversed, that is to say that no products should be allowed unless they have been subject to field-testing for over ten years in a controlled environment. This must include both the direct effect of the product and the residual effect on both the treated produce and the surrounding soils and water systems. Only if a chemical can be shown to have no lasting effects over this period or have any trace left in the environment should it be permitted for general use. Industry would no doubt complain bitterly that this would be uneconomic and make the introduction of new products virtually impossible. This might be a problem for the manufacturers but hardly for society.

The same principles apply to the introduction into Europe of GM (Genetically Modified) crops as the limited field tests carried out in the UK have shown that there is little or no benefit in their introduction. The tests were largely inconclusive but the additional yield was marginal. The whole point of these crops is that they have been modified to be unaffected by specific herbicides and pesticides thus enabling the more extensive use of chemicals.

The only winner in this scenario is the manufacturer who would have a guaranteed closed market for their products. The farmers would become even more dependent on both seed supplies and purchasing specific chemicals to ensure an adequate harvest. The fact is that consumers have clearly indicated that they distrust and wish to avoid GM produce. The farmers themselves are concerned that these products will contaminate the older species and as the benefit is very limited there appears to be no valid reason why the UK Government has agreed to allow their partial introduction.

Organic farming is more labour intensive and the crop yields are lower taken over the whole farm. These factors are counter balanced by the reduced costs of purchasing herbicides, pesticides and fertilisers with the end result that Organic farming is slightly more profitable for the farmer once the conversion process is completed.

This period of conversion is allows the land to purge itself of chemicals and enables the soil to regenerate to become naturally fertile and eliminate the dependence on chemical additives. The lower yield is already balanced by the additional value of the crop, simply because at the end of the day consumers will pay more for Organic produce.

The increased labour costs are a fact of life but in a society where technology is creating increases in unemployment this can hardly be sighted as a major disadvantage.
The worst problem is the additional working of the land invariably leads to higher fuel consumption because farmers are not about to revert to working the land with animals.

Department 11, Aude, in France has 3,400 registered farmers operating a total land area of 192,000 Ha, the equivalent of 56 Ha per farmer taken as a simple average. This area is comparable to Somerset in the UK and reflects a typical agricultural area but with considerable local industry. If the estimates for the above unit are averaged over the farm area and then used to calculate the effect on the whole department then the numbers are:

Domestic Use based on 3,400 Farmhouses……..3.6 mtoe (42 Twh)
Domestic Heating……………………………….8.1 mtoe (94 Twh)

Guestimate for Chemical production.............. 5 mtoe (61 Twh)
Diesel for Farm Use...................................8.6 mtoe (100 Twh)

Estimated loss to society............................46 mtoe (532 Twh)

Unfortunately the numbers cease to have comprehensible significance for most people but the reality is that the estimated diesel usage for the farms in the Aude is 14.4 million litres annually. However these numbers are presented, the final effect is inescapable: the volumes used are very large.

It is also an indisputable fact that under a century ago the agricultural system was fully sustainable and that this change plays a major role in the overall pollution levels.

It is practical to operate diesel engines on vegetable oil so if the farmers produced sufficient oil producing crops then it would be feasible to return to a sustainable system. The crop yield for sunflower is theoretically 4.5 Ton per Ha of produce or around 2,000 L sunflower oil per Ha (equivalent to 24.6 Mwh per ha). Theoretically the farmer could run his machinery on sunflower oil just as well as commercial diesel but the seeds would need pressing. Realistically he could assume a return of 1,500 L per Ha to allow for the processing so needing 2 Ha of land set aside for oil production to meet the diesel requirements for the farm machinery. He would become dependent on obtaining a good yield from the crop but this would be a sustainable solution.

It is interesting to note that 3 Ha set aside for animal fodder and grazing would be sufficient to keep approximately four horses throughout the year, which happens to be just the number required to operate the farm historically.

If you set aside a further 3 Ha of land, you could also produce sufficient gas-oil to provide domestic heating in the winter months, thus making the whole farm unit become self-sufficient. Any small additional surplus of fuel could be used for domestic transport but once the vehicle leaves the agricultural property, it becomes subject to the fuel tax controls imposed by central government.

The cost of the sunflower oil would be approximately 25 c per l or just under half the current price of agricultural gasoil. In Europe, agricultural fuel has minimum tax and retails at around 60c per L against a current price, 2006, for car fuel at 1.08 E. This change would also reduce the agricultural production of food for the consumer which could lead to an overall food shortage. This is a part of the overall problem which simply relates to the population numbers and enhances the logic that there should be a considered and planned policy of overall population decrease.

The incoming sun's radiation calculated at 1 kw per m2 for 7 hours a day is the equivalent to 29,200 Mwh Per ha so the conversion ratio for sunflower oil works out at just under 1%. This is due in part because the sunflowers are only grown between the end of April and August thus utilising only part of the sun's energy available over the whole year and in part because the plant also has to grow using a major part of the incoming energy to create the stem ,leaves and the remainder of the seed.

Alternatively if the farmer placed solar panels on the field the energy conversion rate could be over 12% so a complete Ha of panels (10,000 M2) would produce 3,500 Mwh in a full year. These panels would have to be aligned to the sun throughout the day but this is the equivalent of around 265,000 l gas-oil.

Realistically it would be impractical to cover the field completely with panels, the maximum coverage that would be practical would be under 50% so in effect the farmer would still need to set aside 2 Ha of land, but in this case he would be making a significant contribution to the overall energy needs of the country.

The farmer has fallow land set aside each year of at least 5% of the farm area. The intention is this land is allowed to rest during the year so that the soil can regenerate whilst the land provides a haven for the local insects and wildlife. The land should not be farmed but if solar panels were placed on part of the land this would not detract from the benefits of leaving the land fallow.

The majority of agricultural properties in the Aude also have the additional energy source from the wind in the area. A wind turbine here can be expected to produce rated power for in excess of 2,000 hours pa with the result that a 1.5 Kw rated turbine should generate over 3 Mwh pa. In effect, just four turbines of this size would provide over 50% of the annual agricultural power requirements for the property. A combination of the two would virtually restore the property to self sufficiency in energy terms.

Large scale grid connected solar "farms" have been built around the world over the last few decades and these have proved operationally and technically practical. The fundamental drawback is that the peak power is produced on sunny summer days and no power is generated during the long winter nights. These are typically rated at 300 Kw to 500 Kw (500 Kw Phalk- Mont Soleil Switzerland estimated annual output 700 Mwh Pa from 4,575 m2 of solar arrays). These installations are also built in Germany, Italy, France and Spain and now make a contribution to the European energy system.

A feasibility study for a large solar array installation over several square kilometres has been prepared in conjunction with the Saudi and German Governments in which the electricity generated is converted to Hydrogen, liquefied and transported to Germany to replace hydrocarbon fuels. The proposal is uneconomic partly because of the costs of liquefaction and transportation to Germany, but also because of on-site management problems of operating and maintaining a site of this size in the middle of the Arabian Desert.

Ignoring the financial calculations, it must be advantageous for farmers to return to self sufficiency and cut their annual fuel bills to nothing. In real terms this will return agriculture to the historical basis where farmers are not only self sufficient but have a proportion of their income from energy sales to the community in general. The scenario outlined above is intended to create the situation where farmers become independent in energy terms both for the agricultural operations but also for the domestic requirements of the farm dwellings.

Once the system is functioning based on dual fuel use for existing tractors and generation of high electrical power demands by reciprocating internal combustion engines, then manufacturers will produce hydrogen designed equipment. This equipment will invariably involve the use of fuel cells to provide both electrical power needs and to power vehicles. In practice the tractor will become the generator for high power requirements as well as the mechanical work horse for the agricultural operations.

The simple reality is that the dramatically higher efficiency of this type of equipment will cut the power demand by virtually 50%. The farmer will then be in a position to sell the surplus power to the local community and create a cash income simply on the back of the increased efficiency of new equipment.

.

The loop is then closed and farmers should be in a position to produce food economically, without the need for subsidies to hold prices down. In effect the historic farm animals and trees will be replaced by solar panels and wind turbines and the cash crop has changed from firewood to pure hydrogen. The farmer is in the position of having no expenditure in respect of energy, which for the original example of a 40 Ha unit represents an annual saving of at least 5,000 Euros at current energy prices with an additional cash income of approximately the same value.

The farmer would be thus at least 10,000 Euros better off, which is directly comparable to the maximum level of existing farm subsidies. The economy would gain because the balance of payments improvement because oil imports would be reduced by the equivalent of at least 7,000 l diesel and probably more because part of the electricity consumed previously is generated from hydrocarbon fuels.

If each farm built a 1.4kw hydro electric plant, equivalent to a domestic vacuum cleaner in size and power, operating for 300 days a year – allowing for maintenance and low rainfall – then this would produce a total of 10 MWh pa or the equivalent of 1000 Litres of tractor fuel.   On the same basis if 25m² of solar panels were installed then these would also produce the same 1000 Litres of Tractor fuel. It becomes a simple calculation to change farming to net energy producers which would in itself eliminate the need for any farm subsidies.

The environment would gain immeasurably especially if the change in energy use was paralleled by a conscious decision to reduce dependence on chemical pesticides and herbicides.

Grants are already available in various formats across Europe that would be payable to encourage the installation of sustainable energy generation. These could easily be extended to meet a substantial part of the initial capital cost of the installation, especially if they were linked to a permanent reduction in farm subsidies for the individual participating farms. The farmer would gain from the independence of individual energy production, producing savings comparable to the loss of the subsidy. Most people involved in agriculture accept that subsidies will have to be phased out in the future and this would be one way in which farmers could stabilise their position and eliminate the longer term concerns over the removal of agricultural subsidies.

Society would have to find capital investment at a time when government expenditure already exceeds income. This should be treated as a capital investment in the fundamental infrastructure of the country and as such, should be funded by long term borrowing rather than current year expenditure. In reality, each installed system will be at least 50% local manufacturing and there is no reason why the whole of the system cannot be sourced nationally, and as far as Europe is concerned, certainly from within the EU. The result is that the capital investment will result in a direct increase in local employment reducing government current account expenditure whilst at the same time increasing government income with additional tax revenues. The fact that the capital investment is offset in the longer term by the cessation of farm subsidy payments can only be to the long term benefit of the exchequer and thus society.

The fact is that the fossil fuel bonanza has resulted in dramatic changes in agricultural practices, which does make these practices either correct or advantageous to society.

The rising costs of both direct fuel and manufactured products has pushed farmers into the situation where farming has become uneconomic. There is a practical and positive solution which can be implemented that will undo the damage caused by the changes over the last few decades. It would be a simple matter for farmers to not only become self-sufficient, but become significant contributors for the whole country's energy means which simply requires a change of attitude and policy.

The same argument applies to the fishing industry where the UE fisheries policy has been ridiculed for the last decades but it has achieved a stabilisation and now growth in fish stocks. However the fishing industry is clearly struggling with many fishermen unable to catch sufficient to produce a realistic economic return. In essence this comes down to the fuel costs now associated with fishing with the net result that the fish caught frequently do not even cover the fuel costs expended to effect the catch. If fishermen were able to fuel their boats from independently owned sources then this situation would disappear. It is unlikely that fishermen will return to sailing vessels but it would be feasible for them to change to vessels fuelled indirectly by tidal or wind power thereby reducing their running costs dramatically.

The end game is rational and easy to envisage but the conversion from the current situation will take a major change in Government approach and substantial capital investment.

1 WWF & Co-Operative Bank –http://www.co-operativebank.co.uk/cwc or tina.skar@wwfus.org

Chapter 7
Usage

The core question can be evolved -- Has human activity developed to the extent that there are measurable changes both to the planets systems and human society making the future uncertain. Assuming this danger exists then is there a solution that will reverse the changes within a time scale that will mitigate or resolve the conflicts.

The vast consumption of hydrocarbon fuel has driven the expansion of society to the point where there are measureable changes to the eco system. The failure of human society, predominantly in the developed world, is likely and due more to financial collapse due to escalating fuel prices rather than an absolute unavailability of fuel.

In perspective, the developed countries have used about 50% of the hydrocarbon oil deposits on the planet and gas in the last 50 years. The rate of consumption has exploded exponentially over this very short timescale with the result that supply will decrease as demand continues to increase leading to a dramatic rise in price and availability only to a progressively limited few. Post the Second World War, personal motorised transport was limited to the aristocracy and domestic energy use limited to light and cooking in towns and cities, with no TV or domestic appliances.

The time scale for the creation of the current problem is around fifty years, even though a major part of this escalation took place over just thirty years, so realistically the time scale for resolution and correction should be shorter. In essence an equally massive reduction must be achieved over the next ten years; this will require consensus and determination from the populations and their governments.

The required reduction in non sustainable energy use needs to be 80%. I would like to pretend that this is a carefully calculated assessment but it is merely a compromise between the ideal of 100% and the inadequacy of an overall reduction of 60%. This can only be achieved in two ways, the reduction in energy use and the provision of sustainable energy capture systems to provide for society.

The first and most obvious requirement to reduce consumption is a planned and consistent reduction in the number of consumers. In the UK this would be of the order of a 15 million reduction down to a stable population of around 50 million. This is approaching a 20% reduction and would have a massive impact on the stability and security within society but needs to be achieved across the whole world population. It would also eliminate the current pressure on housing stocks, water supply and provision of food.

The ancient texts that form the basis of all religions and cultures in the world imply or even require a system of consistent reproduction but it must be considered that when these texts were written the survival of human society was dependent on consistent and enhanced birth rate. Human society was subject to high levels of child mortality and a life expectancy at best of three score years and ten so that a high birth rate gave a slow growth of the population in times of plenty. This provided a buffer against natural events in the form of pestilence or climatic events that caused periods of higher mortality so that society could continue. Today the reverse is true with modern medicine cutting child mortality and increasing life expectancy to the extent that it is now the size of the population that puts human existence at risk.

I do not intend to have a theological or philosophical consideration of reproduction but it is logical that if human advances have disrupted and modified the natural balance of the population then parallel advances in education and birth control should be equally advanced to redress this imbalance. It is apparent that the birth rate in developed society stabilises with education combined with the availability of birth control.

The current political pressure to control immigration reflects the general understanding that public services cannot be funded within a balanced budget and that any increase in population compounds this problem. It is ridiculous to continue to fund day to day public expenditure with long term debt.

The Chinese state has tackled this fundamental problem head on, resulting in discussions on human rights, but they have understood the problem and put in place measures to contain their own population growth. I do not pretend to agree with their policies in principle but population growth must be contained and immediately, this will never be an easy path; but ignoring the logic is potentially disastrous

The natural ecosystems have an unfortunate and consistent ability to redress imbalances, we simply do not fully understand the complexity of the inter relationships both for the environment and the life cycles on the planet. Whether the natural systems will create the changes necessary to redress the explosion of human population is unknown but the potential for the rapid spread of any untreatable and contagious disease is inherently available in the movement of individuals around the globe. The speed of movement minimises the time available for the medical research to provide a cure.

Equally the dependence of the developed countries on centralised power generation and distribution combined with the long distance transport essential to maintain food and water supplies makes any significant disruption of these potentially devastating. These are vulnerable to disruption by both human conflict, even terrorism, or environmental events.

In the past years we have recorded extremes in temperature, both high and low, and storm systems. Global warming is probable the wrong wording as this implies a consistent (and slow) rise in temperature but in reality what we are experiencing is extremes both in cold and hot temperatures. This increased range is generating larger storm systems and significant climatic changes resulting in drought or flooding equally.

Perception of the significance and effects of what seems to be a marginal increase in average temperatures appears to be discounted by many. Humans naturally live in a narrow temperature range between 10 & 25° C with this extended significantly by applied technology. Within this context an increase in summer temperatures of 1° C does appear superficially to be a minor change.

A small swimming pool losses water at a rate of about 1mm a day in the winter period but by between 3 & 4mm a day in the summer months when the water temperature rises by up to 5º C. In simplistic terms the loss increases by 2-3mm or 0.05mm per degree increase in temperature. For a 10m² swimming pool this equates to three and a half mm of evaporation for every degree rise in water temperature per week. This is 35 litres (or 35Kg) of water a week for every one degree rise in temperature.

This swimming pool will certainly not change the environment but the bigger one which stretches off the coast of West Africa even considered at 2000 Km² and will put 10 Billion Kg of extra water into the atmosphere every day. This is the cause of increased rainfall and major storm systems which are causing damage and flooding. As this additional water rises through the atmosphere energy is transferred from the surface and is the driving force within the storm systems. These can arbitrarily flip into instability which are experienced as hurricanes or tornadoes.

All this ignores the potential for significant geological events that could immediately compound the effects of human activity on the environment and create an immediate and devastating environmental change that would, in the very short term, change human survival. The potential for a massive geological event is compromised, in human perception, by the last few hundred years of relative stability but in geological timescales this is no more than an instant. The records include two major events in the last two hundred years and analysis of geological records indicate at least one life changing event in the last 5,000 years. We are blind where it comes to predicting or even really understanding geological events, so the timescale is completely open.

The change from the historical diverse and self sufficient growth in population to a society dependent on external sources of transport and centralised energy distribution make current lifestyle potentially fragile.

The potential rise in sea levels will displace human activity in all sea level cities and areas but there is no clear idea of timescale as every year the ice caps melt more which results in faster melting in subsequent years.

The sources of oil and gas are predominately located in areas of the world that are politically and culturally hostile to the main consumers and these areas have in the main local instability if not outright civil war. The potential for significant disruption of either the sources or the extended transport links is high and either would result in major shortages in the main consumer countries.

Domestic energy consumption accounts for approximately 40% of total energy use in the developed world but if commercial energy use is also included this increases to over 55%. In reality commercial use is very similar to domestic use in that the majority of the energy is utilised to maintain public areas in shops and offices and non industrial workplaces at comfortable temperatures with adequate lighting. The energy calculations are different mainly due to the fact that the majority of these building operate during normal working hours but are predominately vacant during the night.

The improvements in personal transport efficiency over the last decade have been dramatic but driven by escalating fuel costs. It is unlikely that similar improvements can be achieved going forward but changes in perception could still radically reduce personal transport fuel costs if full hybrid or full electric vehicles were used for localised short trips.

If you consider a simple vehicle journey that starts from rest, accelerates to say 50Km/Hr and then slows down to rest again. If this Journey requires an energy input of 10KWh, or approximately 1 litre of fuel, then say the acceleration uses 7 KWh and the steady speed uses the balance of 3KWh.

If this journey is powered by a fully electric vehicle then the energy input will be 10 KWh from the battery but approximately 3KWh will be returned to the battery during the slowing process. The net energy use will thus be 7 KWh.

If this is a traditional vehicle the journey will use 10 KWh to the start of the slowing and then an additional usage during the slowing process. But as this is the energy converted into movement so is the output from the engine, but as the engine is less than 50% efficient then the fuel used will be over 2 Litres or 21 KWh. Thus there is the potential to reduce usage by 66%.

As such most of the following sections apply directly to commercial use and similar savings could be achieved.

If a typical domestic unit, 160 m² for four persons, is considered then the annual consumption of electricity for low power appliances calculates at around 1000 Kwh. This power gives us the convenience of lights at the press of a switch, TV, stereo and the now mandatory computer with the majority of this power consumed by lighting.

The first and easiest opportunity for moving towards a sustainable lifestyle is the reduction in lighting use internally and having automatically controlled external lights either by time clock, photocell or both. The most dramatic reduction can be achieved by simply changing all light bulbs to energy efficient types. It is a fundamental fact that a filament light bulb only converts 15% of the energy to light with the balance as heat. Everyone knows a normal light bulb is uncomfortably hot to touch even if only on for a few minutes. The modern energy saving bulbs consumes 20% of the power for the same luminosity so a 60w filament bulb can be changed for an 11w incandescent one with absolutely no reduction in light. This simple change will reduce lighting power use to a fifth of the current use. This has over the last five years become accepted and is now mandatory in many countries.

The multitude of electronic equipment filling our houses must also be brought into the low power consumption estimates and these have been assumed to use 420Kwh pa. It is a simple matter to estimate this, take the power rating for each separate unit, multiply this by the number of hours used every day and then multiply this by 365 to get an annual total. In terms of the design for an alternative an estimate must be made of both the mean and the maximum consumption on a daily basis.

The major energy use for individuals is domestic heating, or cooling in hotter climates, but this energy use can be drastically cut by installation of modern insulation. A well insulated property consumes less than a fifth of the energy used in a poorly insulated property which enables major savings to be realised by upgrading domestic units.

It is interesting to note that BP, one of the worlds foremost oil companies, has invested in solar energy research for the last fifty years and are now a major manufacturer of a complete range of solar panels and associated equipment. In the last few years some of the new BP petrol stations have grown solar panels, discretely above the petrol pump canopy, a few even have wind turbines, and these collectors provide power for the operation of the service station. This is more than a simple research exercise for BP Solar, and certainly not a publicity stunt, there is no information on site or accessible details explaining or promoting these stations. This can only be a considered business operation, which not only reduces their overhead costs but also provides the opportunity to maintain supplies even in the event of a power cut. A cynic might say that only an oil company could discretely install this type of system to give themselves a competitive edge and independence whilst the rest of the population remains dependent on their oil products.

If a hypothetical residential unit of four people is considered in Brighton, on the South Coast and they require One KWh to cook a meal in the oven. If this power is produced by Solar panels on their roof or by local wind or tidal systems then the energy consumed is fractionally over One KWh.

However if this energy is generated in a coal powered station in the midlands then the power station needs to generate 1.5 KWh to allow for the average transmit ion losses within the UK. Again the Power station is only 40% efficient so the steam boiler requires 3.33 KWh of input coal energy. This coal is now mined in Australia, transported to a bulk Carrier and navigated half way round the globe, and then unloaded and transported to the Power station. This results in a requirement to mine at least 4.2 KWh of coal from the mine to produce the 1KWh in Brighton.

Unfortunately the same applies if the electric car is recharged from the power station in the midlands. In this case there is no environmental benefit in having an energy efficient vehicle that is non polluting – all that happens is the pollution is produced elsewhere.

The same argument applies to the Farmer who uses 1,000 litres of fuel – he actually gets optimistically 500 litres worth of useable work out of the fuel so that his micro hydro station is realistically worth 2,000 litres of fuel. This does assume that he uses the power generated at 90% efficiency so effectively has to utilise an electric tractor.

There is currently serious concern in all major cities at the level of Nitrogen Oxides polluting the atmosphere. This is blamed on Diesel cars and there is no doubt that these do produce more nitrogen oxides than petrol cars, but the operative word here is more. Any fuel combusted at high temperature will produce some nitrogen oxides and if the pressure of the combustion is also high then the proportion produced will rise but petrol cars and even domestic gas boilers will produce this pollution.

The major issue is CO^2 and every litre of fuel produces 3.5 Kg of emission, this might seen relatively small until the quantity of fuel is considered. This is the essential cause of the damage to the atmosphere and when this issue is addressed then the other pollution will disappear.

Science clearly states that the energy loss in any energy transfer is proportional to the temperature difference during this transfer. It is impossible to achieve high levels of efficiency when the energy transfer takes place at high temperatures so if we are to move to systems that operate in the 90% efficiency area then these have to be effected at close to normal temperature. This is an inescapable reality which cannot be avoided and virtually imposes the direct use of electricity to provide for the needs of society.

The consumption of this hypothetical unit, based on 112 KWh per day /person would be over 12,000 KWh per month at a cost of £2,400 which would certainly be an unacceptable electricity bill. The figure is however close to the actual cost of all living expenses for this unit.

This figure for average personal consumption is quite frightening especially as this is based on the UK consumption figures but if you take N America the figure is 20% higher and all these figures exclude the energy utilised to manufacture all the goods imported into the developed world.

Even more frightening is the one billion individuals on the planet existing on between one and two KWh per day and this figure includes the biomass energy consumed, this is engineering speak for malnutrition and starvation. This clearly demonstrates the vast difference between the developed world who consume about 50 times the overall energy available to the poorest. Even those in the 2 to 4 KWh band, and these account for the next two billion people, are only just above basic subsistence living level and having a negligible effect on the world eco-system but are paying more than their fair share of the cost and damage caused by Global worming.

The difference between overall consumption and actual usage is significant across all developed societies but if this is reduced down to a difference of around 10% then the overall consumption figure can be cut by more than 50% overall. This inherently requires energy to be produced locally, within ten miles, and managed locally. This locality needs to be considered on a Parish by Parish basis with all individuals in each section jointly responsible for their own energy usage and production.

Personal independence can be achieved by installing solar panels both for personal use with any immediate surplus transferred locally. In classical financial terms it is not cost effective but with the current price levels of consumer energy constantly rising and taking a realistic view of the lifespan of the solar panels at over 50years the difference is very marginal. Once the system is in place then the energy price is effectively fixed for the next decades. This is the real financial justification with energy costs annually escalating at between 5% and 12% any capital investment that fixes energy costs in absolute terms becomes financially beneficial within a short time.

This type of system involves a significant initial capital expenditure but there are grants or subsidies available in most European countries for both solar and energy investments which would significantly reduce the initial investment. The physical installation is not complex or difficult but if the system was independently installed then the installation cost would significantly increase the initial costs. The only way to asses the real costs for a specific project is to evolve a design and then search for the best prices and any grants available.

The electricity companies are now compelled to allow an integrated connection of individual power systems to the grid. In this case any surplus power produced in the home is sold to the electric company. Simply because of the instantaneous nature of electricity this is of limited benefit to the generating companies and they only pay a small fraction of the retail price they charge for electricity but this is enhanced by government subsidies. This is not simply a negative policy on behalf of the generating companies but reflects the fundamental need to store energy for later use. Generated power has no value unless you have an instantaneous demand to match it. The fundamental problem is storing the energy for later use. As soon as this energy is transferred over significant distances then the transmitting losses come into play thereby reducing the value of the power generated.

The world needs to rationalise energy consumption but there is the potential to cut consumption to around the net usage of energy by introducing systems that are 90% efficient. This would reduce consumption by half at a stroke and this combined with population planning and management could result in an overall reduction in current levels of consumption of at least 60%. This has to involve localised energy generation with a sustainable form of energy storage.

Chapter 8
Hydrogen

Extracting the energy from the environment in a fully
sustainable way is not particularly difficult and certainly does
not use any ultra new technology or innovative breakthroughs.
The fundamental reason that every property in Europe is not
automatically equipped to be energy independent is simply
that the incoming energy not only does not fit in conveniently
with demand but rather that it is generally available in periods
of minimal demand. The trick is to have the energy available
when required so electrical energy must be converted to
another form so that it can be stored.

Hydrogen is fundamental and integral in the energy produced
by our sun and is the key to the existence of the cosmos in
which we occupy an insignificant segment. Engineers have
always known that a move to a hydrogen energy system is
logical and achievable but this has been overlooked because of
the apparently cheap and easy availability of hydrocarbon fuel.

This situation has evolved in the past seventy or so years since
the general availability of centralised power based on cheap
fossil fuel sources. Prior to this every household was
independent and either had to purchase fuel in the form of
wood, candles or oil or they were net producers. This change
over from sustainable existence to total dependence on
hydrocarbon fuels has created the perception that energy is
available on demand without thought or planning. Now as the
price of centralised energy soars higher, and the probability of
real shortages looms, consumers have lost the knowledge to

be independent. Only a century ago all the primary energy was derived from the sun, today renewable sources account for less than 10% of our consumption.

The suns energy falls evenly across the earth's surface so it is only logical that the energy capture should be equally spread out; The fossil fuel bonanza must be considered as an unfortunate blip in human development and the time has already passed to return to a more balanced and equal energy regime.

Storage is the fundamental issue with all renewable energy whether for a few hours to give continuity in supply or capturing the summer surplus to provide for the cold and bleak winter. Even storing a few tons of logs takes up space, ideally close to the fireplace, which conflicts almost invariably with the leisure or service areas adjoining the house. Most people using solid fuel end up with two stores, a small convenient one for topping up during the day and evening and the main store located out of the way covered against the elements.

Electricity has always been impossible to store, it is simply an immediate source of energy, fundamental to its nature, Electrical power is simply electrons moving along the wires and these cannot be collected for later use. The storing large numbers of electrons is impossible and the effect is clearly demonstrated every time a lightening bolt crosses the skies. If the primary energy is generated electricity then any immediate surplus must be converted to another form of energy instantaneously.

A rechargeable battery simply converts the electrical energy during charging into chemical energy later this chemical energy is dissipated when power is taken from the battery in the form of electrical power. The batteries themselves deteriorate with time, every car owner knows that the battery will need replacing every four years or so, adding to the running costs of the system. The new batteries appearing in Hybrid Cars are a dramatic step forward both in terms of energy stored and long life but are totally inadequate to consider as a major energy storage medium.

The solution is to convert electricity into hydrogen. This gas can be stored and used when required as a primary fuel for gas burning appliances and to produce electricity as required in fuel cells.

Energy transfer is fundamental and essential for all life to exist and now human society is totally dependent on the manipulation of energy from one form to another to provide the environment which is now required by consumers. The adsorption of sunlight in plants provides the source of all food on the planet and without this energy transfer then life would cease to exist. Modern society tends to discount the significance of this but it has not only provided for the survival of all species but has created all the fossil fuel deposits that we are currently squandering.

The move to a hydrogen based system appears radical initially but in reality we are already totally dependent on hydrogen as our primary source of energy. Hydrocarbon fuels are simply utilising the carbon atoms to transport the hydrogen – the energy released by hydrocarbon fuels comes primarily and most significantly from the hydrogen combining with air to produce water. This energy provides everything from domestic heating and cooking to transport and even the information transmitted in our communication networks. Modern society would cease to function without mobile phones let alone a water supply or transported food.

The only external source of energy for the Earth comes from the sun, at the rate of 17,000 times current human consumption, and this drives and provides for all life. This energy is adsorbed by plants and organisms both on land and in the oceans and they provide the starting point for all life. Photosynthesis is taught, initially as an introduction to the carbon cycle, from an early age but in reality the fundamental point is overlooked.

This is where the fantastic nano technology kicks in: A single photodynamic cell in a plant adsorbs sunlight and utilise this energy to dismantle the Carbon dioxide adsorbed through the cell wall but concurrently it dismantles the water molecules adsorbed through the roots. The cell nucleus holds the magic control programme which manages the construction of organic molecules required by the cell. These can be as simplistic as to make cellulose for addition cell walling or to create a duplicate of the cell nucleus – thereby allowing the cell to duplicate itself by division into two parts. These organic compounds are constructed atom by atom under the constant control of this programme. Literally the cell takes one carbon atom and assembles this with hydrogen atoms and other carbon atoms to fabricate each molecule required by the control programme whether this is for the direct objective of duplicating the individual cell or for the benefit of the whole organism. This enables plats to both grow and then subsequently to produce the seeds or cells necessary for the plant to duplicate itself in the next growing season.

Some organisms are unable to utilise the suns energy directly so these obtain their energy by dismantling the energy locked into the cells consumed as food. This whole system works because the plant species produce surplus sugars & carbohydrates together with the vitamins etc which are consumed by the animal species. The food products are dismantled by releasing the hydrogen and combining this with oxygen to produce water and energy. These animals also create carbon (dioxide) waste, plus limited energy, but primarily the energy is produced by water production.

This energy transfer not only enables each species to grow and thrive but with the secrets held within the DNA control programme these enable each organism to create an image of itself. This is the secret of life and is totally dependent on the transfer of energy from solar electromagnetic radiation to molecular manipulation under the complete control and management of the DNA programme. All of this is fundamentally reliant on the energy associated with the water molecule both to dismantle it or re-combine it--- life depends on this energy.

It is clear that every cell within every organism is able to communicate so that the complete organism has the building blocks necessary to sustain the life of the organism and then start the reproduction cycle enabling each organism to create a future generation in the image of itself. This reproduction is essentially the movement of the DNA control programme forward to the next generation.

In essence the natural systems rely on the conversion of the incoming energy from the Sun to the dismantling of water molecules to provide atomic hydrogen. Human technology is primitive in comparison and we are incapable of duplicating the natural order for our own objectives but we are capable of utilising the fundamental process of producing molecular hydrogen. We can utilise this as a fuel source which would be wholly sustainable and as such fully reversible.

When plant leaves adsorb sunlight simple observation shows that they do not become hot. In fact plants have a cooling effect restricting temperature rise on the ground surface and below the leaf canopy. In essence this adsorption is an endothermic process with plants both utilising the suns radiation but also obtaining heat energy from the surroundings. Simplistically this process is 100% efficient and carried out at atomic level.

The natural systems therefore rely on both diversity of energy collectors in every plant leaf and a completely efficient energy conversion system.

The solution for human society is to convert electricity into hydrogen. This gas can be stored and used when required as a primary fuel produced by electrolysis. This process breaks apart the chemical bond in water between the Hydrogen and

Oxygen atoms releasing both gasses. The chemical bond in water is exceptionally strong and considerable energy is required to break the atoms apart. Conversely the same energy is released when these atoms are rejoined either by combustion or in a fuel cell.

The science and technology are well understood and established and the process is efficient with over 90% of the input electrical energy being stored in the captured Hydrogen. The electrolysis cell is in itself a simple device similar in size and appearance to a car battery but with two separate gas release tubes one for the Hydrogen and the other for the Oxygen. If the Hydrogen is to be utilised for normal domestic use then the oxygen can simply be released into the atmosphere; is only necessary to collect this gas for advanced fuel cells or other specialised uses. It is prudent in any case to allow the oxygen to escape into the atmosphere as it avoids the potential danger of having both gasses compressed in close proximity to each other. Pure oxygen and hydrogen are the basis of rocket fuel, graphically demonstrating both the potential power and danger of the two gasses together.

Each individual cell has a low input voltage and a specific current flow to achieve high efficiency. In essence systems need to be constructed to mimic the natural world with large numbers of small individual cells all linked together.

It is essential that the Hydrogen is kept pure with no mixing with either the air or even more seriously pure oxygen. Hydrogen is a very good fuel with considerable energy released on combustion so a hydrogen – air mixture is dangerous and potentially explosive. This is not to say that the gas is in itself any more dangerous than hydrocarbon fuels such as propane, natural gas or even petrol. It is essential to remember at all times that high energy fuels are all potentially dangerous and must be handled with extreme care.

It is, however, accepted firstly that Hydrogen was the substantial component of Town and Coal gas happily supplied to houses across the world only a few decades ago through rusting steel pipes and secondly that the modern gas mains and fittings would deal with low pressure hydrogen without modification . The safety regulations and codes of practice applicable to any gas installation must be applied equally stringently to a hydrogen gas system. Assuming that every installation meets these criteria then a Hydrogen based energy system is safer that the current natural gas as it is virtually impossible to develop a gas build up.

If reasonable precautions are taken then the conversion of sustainable energy into hydrogen gas is ridiculously simple. It is not particularly difficult to construct an electrolysis cell and anyone with the appropriate scientific background can easily find the technical information necessary to fabricate a cell. In practice it is easier to just purchase one of the currently manufactured units that are available for both small domestic use up to major commercial plants with outputs ranging from 4 l per hour (max rating 200w) up to 400 l /hr max rating 200Kw.

A recent development is the combined electrolysis cell and fuel cell which not only provides a ready made hydrogen generator but is combined with a fuel cell which provides electrical power when insufficient energy is available from the renewable generators.

The crux of the energy storage is not so much whether hydrogen can be produced but the ability to safely store this gas both in small quantities for basic domestic use and in significant quantities to meet the major winter usage for domestic heating. The efficiency of the systems becomes as important as the fuel when considering the consumption and the availability of energy to meet the demands of users. It is essential that only highly efficient appliances are used to cut the overall consumption to balanced and realistic levels.

The change over to a hydrogen economy would utilise the entire existing infrastructure in both local electricity distribution and gas mains, facilitating the change. In practice hydrogen gas can be mixed with natural gas, up to 15% by volume, without any significant difference for the consumer so allowing a smooth change over from the existing natural gas to Hydrogen as production increases. The existing natural gas mains are equally suited to either gas so any hydrogen produced can already be fed into the gas supply system immediately.

If the hydrogen is to be stored for a long period then the gas is more easily compressed to around 50 atmospheres and stored in high pressure steel tanks. There is no good reason for using a high pressure tank except the reduction in space achieved by so doing. Pressurising the gas requires specially designed pumps and the tank must be designed and rated for the storing of high pressure fuel gas so there is a significant cost involved but the decision comes down to the available space on the property. Properties with good garden areas can easily accommodate both short and long term storage tanks but these would be inconvenient for smaller properties and within built up urban areas.

The longer term solution would be simply to feed the hydrogen into the local utility gas main enabling the user to only retain a small volume of self made hydrogen for immediate use with any surplus sold to the utility company through the supply meter. When user demand is high they would just draw off the main at the normal commercial price. Clearly the utility company would only pay a proportion of the end user cost for hydrogen supplied to the main but the user would eliminate the need for pressurised storage with a substantial capital saving for the installation.

Equally important this system would be applicable to built up urban areas thus enabling all but those living in blocks of apartments to become self sufficient in energy. In this situation only a limited volume of hydrogen would be retained at each property, which from a physiological point of view would almost certainly be considered a safer and more controlled option.

It realistic to produce hydrogen locally now from under utilised renewable generators and feed this directly into the existing gas mains up to the 15% limit (Evan Orr Electronics& Power 1985). This would have the effect of immediately reducing greenhouse gas emissions from gas appliances. When local production approaches the 15% limit small areas of the gas main could be steadily converted to 100% hydrogen.

This is the same principle as selling electricity back to the generating companies except that with a gas supply there is no daily peak tariff or discounted rates. All producers should therefore expect to achieve a price of at least 50% of the end user cost for hydrogen supplied. The utility company will in many cases be selling the user back his own hydrogen so their function is to collect the gas and provide medium term storage.

In order for this to become a practical reality then the gas supplied in a particular area has to be reconverted back to hydrogen. Specialised meters need to be installed to allow the two way flow of gas but with control equipment built in to ensure that only pure hydrogen was passed into the mains. In practical terms this is no obstacle but a dramatic change in attitude would be needed from both the existing energy companies and the politicians. Essentially each householder would not only be an energy consumer but could also be a producer and this would totally disrupt the current status quo both in terms of the tax structure and the effective monopoly on energy supply.

The gas utility company would need medium term storage, these would be gas-o-meters that were common around most towns in the era of Town Gas. In operation they are the same as the storage system outlined above with the gas retained under a water envelope which expands and contracts as the supply and consumption varies. The old tanks have proved very difficult to decommission because of noxious and lethal tars deposited in the sealing water tank. This situation will not occur with pure hydrogen because these tars were produced form volatile compounds present in the coal which escaped into the town gas during the manufacturing process.

The energy companies would see a reduction in turnover due in part to energy savings and in part to each householder's demand being supplied from their own energy producing equipment. Reduction in turnover is fundamentally not good for continued profit growth. The government would suffer reduced tax revenues due to the substantially lower energy use and if hydrogen cars became readily available then no doubt home produced fuel would be very attractive to the consumer. This must be the way forward but it will take a degree of social and political foresight.

The argument from proponents of hydrogen is that it should remain tax free because the tax is only necessary on hydrocarbon fuel to force the consumer to minimise consumption and to pay for some of the cost of undoing the damage to the environment. Whether government exchequers will support this view remains to be seen but initially the loss of revenue will be minor.

The process to obtain liquid hydrogen from the gas is straightforward and is achieved by repeatedly compressing the gas and then cooling the compressed gas prior to repeating the compression. Once liquid hydrogen is obtained it can be stored in high pressure and highly insulated steel cylinders and either retained on site or transported for use elsewhere. In this form each four litres of Hydrogen is the equivalent to one litre of petrol although the weight of the liquid hydrogen is under half that of petrol. Even so the resultant overall weight of the fuel plus the tank is still higher for liquid hydrogen simply because of the weight, and inevitably the cost, of the steel tanks.

The other main drawback is the very low temperatures associated with liquid hydrogen which not only pose a danger to the inexperienced but are so low as to change the atomic behaviour of materials rendering them fragile and brittle. Specialist materials and storage vessels are required to handle liquid hydrogen as this is stored at high pressures and very low temperature, about 250 c degrees below freezing, and no attempt to store or make liquid hydrogen should be undertaken anyone without full specialised knowledge and experience.

This is in part due to the exceptionally low temperatures especially when the gas is drawn off, that are so low as to change the molecular behaviour of materials. The boiling point of liquid hydrogen at normal atmospheric pressure is 253 c below freezing. The other problem is that because the Hydrogen molecule is so small it can find its way through solid walls rather like a mouse slipping through crack in the wall and the higher the pressure the greater the escape potential.

Metal Hydride tanks offer a more practical alternative for high density storage of hydrogen especially for vehicles and longer term storage. The process is similar to liquefying the gas but the temperatures are much closer to normal. The hydride is a metal or an alloy of metals and the hydrogen molecules simply hide in the spaces within the crystals of the hydride. The metal hydride is placed within a pressure cylinder and hydrogen is pumped in at pressures up to 40 atmospheres, as the hydrogen is adsorbed the hydride gives off heat which has to be conducted away. When the hydrogen is required the hydride will release a small part of the retained gas but this has a cooling effect with the result that the supply falls quickly. This is because the hydride adsorbs heat as the hydrogen is released and it is necessary to heat the hydride to enable it to release further hydrogen. In theory the heat given out when the hydride is charged is the same as the heat required to release the hydrogen but unless the storage cycle is very short it is unlikely that the heat can be stored effectively to be reused.

In practice in any operation where the hydrogen is combusted then the exhaust gasses from the engine or boiler are sufficient to provide this heat energy. A hydride tank will hold virtually the same volume of hydrogen when fully charged as an equivalent volume of liquid hydrogen.

As an example a hydride tank 25 cm in diameter and 120cm long was used by the Billings Energy Corporation in a converted 1975 Pontiac with the original engine modified to run on pure hydrogen. This car had a range of 241 km using 2,4kg of hydrogen with virtually the same performance as the original petrol engine. Clearly a modern engine, especially if designed to run on hydrogen, will achieve a vastly higher range and performance. Even better is to use a fuel cell to convert the encapsulated energy available in the hydrogen gas to electricity and run as an electric vehicle.

Refuelling the hydride tank is achieved by connecting a high pressure, between 10 and 40 atmospheres, supply to the tank and for the example above the tank can be 80% re-charged in fifteen minutes and fully in an hour.

The sequence for individual hydrogen storage is thus initially feeding the gas into low pressure water sealed tanks that should be designed to hold a few average days production. The gas from these tanks can be supplied directly to domestic appliances for heating and cooking. Periodically as the hydrogen in these low pressure tanks reaches their capacity the majority of the gas should be pumped into a high pressure storage tank. This compressed gas can be fed back into the low pressure storage tanks when demand exceeds production thus ensuring a supply of energy for domestic use. Equally the high pressure gas can be utilised to directly recharge Metal Hydride tanks to give additional storage capacity or for use in vehicles.

Any process that involves high pressure compression of the hydrogen gas uses significant energy and this is compounded when the gas or storage medium has to be cooled to remove heat energy. The least work should be done on the hydrogen gas as possible to maximise the overall efficiency of the system and high pressure systems should only be considered when very high fuel energy densities are needed. Metal Hydride tanks do provide a practical and realistic form of energy storage for vehicles. But hydrogen produced in electrolysers can be produced at 40 Bar and this improves the effectiveness of the electrolyser by reducing the volume of the gas on the plates, then there is also no requirement to pressurise the gas after production.

There are significant large steel containers constructed as the towers for every wind turbine and the use of these as storage systems would be a logical way forward thus enabling the continuous use of wind turbines combined with electrolysers to store the surplus energy within the tower.

If the opportunity is available then the excess gas should be supplied directly to the gas main. This is the only practical solution to energy storage in built up urban areas where significant individual storage would be impractical and potentially dangerous.

It is important to consider the overall efficiency of the system rather than the efficiency of each part as well as a realistic balance between low pressure storage at low capital cost and sophisticated high pressure storage in tanks that are both expensive and energy inefficient.

Chapter 9
Economy

There is a consensus that the economy is unstable especially among younger people. The financial crises of 2007/8 has made most sceptical over the financial management of institutions and the large multi-national organisations that have been shown to manipulate the markets for immediate gain.

This has impinged on the political systems across the world but especially in the developed countries, in the main because governments have been forced into Austerity packages in a wide variety of forms. These are universally unpopular with the populations who have seen pensions and public services cut to reduce overall expenditure in an attempt to return to a balanced national budget.

If there was a referendum in the UK at present with the option for an extra £5 Billion to be made available to the National Health Service then there is little doubt that this would have overwhelming support by substantially more than 50% of the electorate. However if the referendum question was "are you (every elector individually) prepared to pay £833 (by Debit/CC within 28 days or by deduction from your pension/ income payments) to fund this extra payment to the NHS" then the result would be a resounding NO. The question is not changing simply the way it is presented.

The fundamental problem is that all developed countries are now funding public expenditure by constantly growing borrowing. If the decisions for austerity were simply a proportional allocation of wealth generated within the economy then the choices would be simply a matter of political choice but this is not the case. The mountain of existing debt is steadily accumulating on the assumption that the younger generations will have to resolve this in the future.

National debt is currently measured as a proportion of GDP which has the effect that if a government runs a deficit in a year, by paying extra to the NHS or defence budgets, then they are justified in increasing borrowing even further. This is a farcical scenario as borrowing is unrelated to Treasury income and as such no consideration is ever taken of the ability to repay or service the debt.

The perception seems to be that the solution to this dilemma is to increase tax rates on the wealthy but this ignores the current high level of current taxation and the contribution made to the Treasury. Consider a well paid executive in the city whose institution allocates a total bonus payment of £100,000, the total direct tax paid over to the Treasury amounts to just over £58,000 and when these funds are spent indirect taxes will take a further £6,000. The net income after all taxation is £24,200 which comes out at a tax rate of 76%. Much the same applies to companies, a company with a declared turnover of £1 Billion has invariably already paid over to the Treasury £200 million in VAT and will pay over a further £130 million in payroll taxation so they have contributed £330 million to the Treasury before any assessment of corporation tax and this is without taking into account local business rates.

The whole concept of measuring the strength and health of any economy based on overall GDP is highly questionable.

Consider a framer who invests in renewable energy sources, solar, wind and micro hydro, and utilises this energy production to produce Hydrogen to drive his new farm equipment. He will end this process with substantial capital investment and debt but not only no fuel bills but a small surplus sold into the local community. In the first decade he will be only marginally better off as the majority of the benefit will be offset against the loan repayments but thereafter he will be more profitable and secure. At the end the only measurable increase in sales will come from the surplus energy sold with the current energy expenditure adsorbed into reducing his costs.

However at present he purchases fuel and energy from local suppliers. Consider the oil refinery that purchases oil, included in overall GDP total that refines the oil into motor fuel. This is then sold to local distributer and then sold to the Farmer and both of these are included in overall GDP. In effect the system includes the same real product at least three times when estimating the overall health of the economy.

If the farmer made these investment choices then GDP in respect of his energy operation would fall by a factor of three to four times which under the current analysis would be a monumental depression and catastrophic. But the reality is that the operation would in fact produce the same output in crops and a small but significant extra energy supply resulting in both the farmer and society being better off.

Electorates have voted against the current systems and the world is experiencing a move to extreme parties, both left and right of the political spectrum, leading to extreme views surfacing. The effect is a radical left wing Greek parliament, the potential for D Trump to be US president and the UK Brexit vote. The Spanish electorate have failed to elect any groups of political parties that can even agree to work together leaving the country effectively ungoverned for the last year. The elections due in France and Germany are likely to produce a radical change in political control that could easily result in a surge to the far right. The electorate is sceptical of all politicians due to a seeming endless string of corruption issues and abuses of privilege that involves all parties.

The UK referendum on membership of the EU typifies the underlying problems. In the end 36% of the electorate voted to leave the EU and 34% to remain but 30% could not be bothered to vote and all 16/17 year olds were excluded despite the reality that they will have to sort out the resulting mess.

The leave campaign was based on statements and promises that were made deliberately to sway the electorate with the full knowledge by all those promoting these ideas that they were unsupportable, unrealistic and in many cases simply lies. On the day of the result several prominent leave campaigners admitted the deception but were simply content that they had achieved the result they wanted. It is hardly surprising that people are disenchanted with the politicians when they are shown to be deceitful and misleading whilst putting personal gain and ambition before any consideration of the country or the actual welfare of the individuals living there.

The one issue that is consistently surfacing is migration into established communities, at present Europe has nearly 4 million displaced individuals pressing and trying to enter the zone. These range from refugees displaced by war to economic migrants who are unable to survive in the originating environment but clearly Europe cannot just allow this level of migration without a significant and detrimental effect on its own citizens.

Migration into the UK splits into three distinct groups. Migration from outside the EU but this can be controlled at any time by the UK government who have over the last decade decided to encourage migration.

Migration by refugees but this is contained and controlled by our EU partners who are holding migrants at or adjacent to the EU Eastern borders and restricting the flow of migrants through continental Europe. The problem within the UK is thus limited to those approved to enter the UK by the government but without camps within the UK. This problem will not diminish until the refugees are in a situation where they can return to their home countries to a satisfactory and safe life. This will require financial investment to improve the facilities and infrastructure to enable a quality of life comparable to that currently experienced in the developed world. This investment will have to be funded and supported by the developed world.

The contentious migration as far as the EU referendum was concerned was the free movement of individuals within Europe. The UE economic system is based substantially on the system evolved and developed in the UK over the last few centuries. Within the UK there is an absolute free trade area with no restrictions but this inherently involves the free movement of individuals within the UK. These two elements are inextricably linked so that individuals have complete freedom of movement from Scotland to anywhere else in the UK in the same way in which there is absolute free movement of goods and services. The UK would cease to function if there were movement restrictions between Glasgow and London and exactly the same situation exists in the UE.

If the UK retains full and complete access to the UE market then the free movement of individuals will remain. If the UK enforces restrictions on free movement of people then there will be restrictions on access to the UE markets – this has been confirmed and stated by all in the UE. If the UK leaves the UE with restricted access to the market then the UK economy will be seriously and detrimentally affected with the result that there will be less funds available to the treasury leading to further cuts in the public purse.

However the concerns of the electorate reflect the underlying view that the UK population is too high and the increase in population numbers is straining all public services, specifically housing, the NHS and education. If there is to be a control and limitation on the population then this is not so much an issue of controlling any one form of migration. A clear statement would be required from the government, supported by the majority of the electorate, that this population reduction was the objective of the British people and supported by clear government policy both educationally and financially.

Population growth slows with improved education but this effect could be enhanced by a public consensus with educational support that population growth was fundamentally detrimental to society. Equally the government could reinforce this by changes to child support funding making it financially detrimental for families with three or more children whilst improving the financial position of those families with two or less.

In the first couple of months there has been a limited effect on the UK economy as a result of the Brexit vote and this is purported as a success by those supporting the UK leaving Europe. The Bank of England admitted at the start of the third month that they had supported the UK financial system with additional funding amounting to £100 Billion. This is £50 Billion for each of the first two months and even with this support the pound has devalued by 15% leading to a notional rise in the UK Stock Exchange. This support needs to be considered in the perspective of the additional support needed by the Health Service now estimated at £1 Billion extra a year. It is hardly surprising that the UK economy has shown little sign of decline with this level of additional support combined with the simple fact that nothing has changed and the UK remains a full member of the EU until a formal notice to leave is completed.

Much was made of the £350 million a week paid to the EU during the campaign but it was always clear that the net contribution to the EU was £120 million a week. This is £6.25 Billion a year so the funding provided to the UK economy amounts to sixteen years payments made within the first two months of the result.

Since the financial crisis from 2007, which caused the UK and the rest of the world to drop into recession, incomes have fallen in real terms by around 10%. There has been low inflation since 2010 which dropped to virtually zero by 2016. Then, following the three year shock of the recession, incomes have grown at the rate of inflation up to 2016 but have continued to grow at the same rate despite even lower inflation.

Inflation has fallen due significantly to the dramatic reduction in interest rates which has cut mortgage payments to a third of the 2006/7 levels. This has provided a boost to individual budgets and enabled many to survive the years following 2008. The fear is that when rates start to move upwards again then the reverse will occur either prompting a rise in repossessions or a significant rise in average wages.

Concurrently the cost of energy has fallen steadily, due in part to the world recession cutting demand combined with additional supplies coming to the market both from the Mid East and by expansion of the extraction from Tar deposits in the Arctic. The price of crude fell from a maximum of 100$ barrel in 2008 to as low as 20$ a barrel in late spring 2016. The price has now risen to an average 45$ a barrel but could easily continue to climb to at least 55$. These changes in crude oil have been reflected in the cost of Gas and these both have resulted in lower energy costs in the UK, again pushing inflation lower.

If you consider a mid late spring 2016 price of Crude at 25$ this was £17.25p a barrel but by end September with the fall in the value of sterling combined with rising crude prices this has escalated to £34.60 a barrel – or just over doubled in six months. This is an increase in a litre of car fuel of 42p/Litre and a likely increase in domestic fuel costs of around 12% fed into the economic system over the next 12 months. This at the same time that food imports will be increased by at least 12% which   must lead to rising and escalating inflation and so lead to pressure on payroll costs. This will impinge on the economy slowly in part because supplies are contracted over extended periods and in part because retailers will be reticent to increase prices too quickly to avoid losing market share.

The reality is that fuel costs relate to production costs and although it will take time for these to reflect in retail sale prices the effect remains. This is simple to understand with agriculture where increased fuel costs at the start of 2017 will affect the produce sent to market at the end of 2017 and the prices in the supermarkets in mid 2018. As farmers are already struggling to operate profitably then either prices must rise or more farmers will simply give up producing, the latter option is detrimental to the long term. Equally as fuel costs increase then this will put pressure on incomes and result in higher employment costs which again will be reflected in retail prices but again this will be over an extended period of time.

There is a "feel Good" factor that affects the way in which people behave and this depends on their confidence and belief in the future combined with their ability to meet their current needs and aspirations on a day to day basis. This is impossible to measure but clearly their ability to live acceptably on their current income and have access to the services and facilities they have grown to expect are fundamental.

The results map of the referendum does seem to reflect the "feel Good" factor rather than a definitive political view on the EU but far more a general dissatisfaction with the government and their policies in those areas that have the perception that they are overlooked or ignored. Whether any of these leave areas really expected a radical change to a right wing Conservative government is both questionable and doubtful.

If the hypothetical unit of four in Brighton is re-considered, the fact is that their combined energy consumption comes out at around 450KWh per day and would result in a farcical electricity bill of about £2,400 per month. However this sum is a very good approximation of the overall cost of providing for four individuals in the SE of the UK on a monthly basis. The fundamental question is whether this is a mathematical coincidence or whether it really reflects the reality of the economy.

If consideration is given to individual energy consumption then clearly any wealth creating individual must generate sufficient income to provide for both the individual and every dependent that is not creating wealth. On this basis then each employed individual needs to generate around 250KWh per day or on the same basis just over £50 per day or £6.25 per hour. This employment assessment includes part time working, so if this is not discounted by 50% then the daily rate rises to £120 per day or £15 per hour. These figures are clearly consistent with the UK economy and reflect the current employment situation. Equally clearly, those on a combined income of less than £50 per day or £1,000 per month will struggle to survive whilst those comfortably above this level will be able to balance their budget.

All these calculations are based on a cost per KWh of 20p but this is a good approximation to the actual cost of domestic energy supply and is consistent with the cost of vehicle fuel, currently at 16p per KWh. The one major inconsistency is the cost of food, which on the basis of a weekly supermarket bill of £80 for these four, produces an average price of £1.15 per KWh. This apparent inconsistency reflects the extra costs of transport, food processing and retailing in food supplies but the food producers actually get paid nearer 15p per KWh for their produce.

There is a clear mathematical link between energy value and money but as with any logical assessment there must be a reality between the mathematic assessment and the reality. At the end of the day all raw materials on the planet were formed at the time of the formation of the solar system and humans exploit these given gifts by extracting minerals and material available within the surface level of the planet. These exist but are not created. The energy we use to change these reserves into materials and so to products we consume all come from the solar energy that is conveniently also provided by our solar system. It is therefore logical to argue that every product utilised by humans has a value proportional to the total energy utilised in its evolution into a definable product. Whether this solar energy is current or historic does not change the logical argument but does change the effect on the environment in which all exist.

This becomes more a philosophical argument then an assessment of the mathematics or science but at the end of the day scientists now understand that energy is the driving force in the natural world and the cosmos, so it is a simple logical step to accept that this is also the driving force in life on our small segment of the universe. If energy is the fundamental currency in the universe is it not reasonable or logical that this should be the fundamental currency in human society.

But again returning to the hypothetical household of four in Brighton we must consider the value of one KWh generated locally by a renewable process in comparison to 1.5KWh produced by the power station in the midlands or the 4 KWh extracted from Australia. So is the locally generated power worth 1,5 times the power from the midlands or even 4 times the value of the coal extracted in Australia. The real problem is that over and above the power wasted in the transmit ion we have the unacceptable fact that the consumption of coal is devastating the environment by carbon pollution. This is a real cost whether this is clearing up after floods in Cumbria or the complete loss of communities in S America. The effect is worldwide and the cost is paid at present either directly by those devastated by climatic extremes or indirectly by all in reduced food supplies to increased insurance premiums.

The reality is that for every Kg of hydrocarbon fuel consumed this creates 3.5Kg of carbon dioxide pollution into the atmosphere and every individual on the planet pays for this pollution. This pollution is the driving force behind climate change and this is escalating on an annual basis, climatologists can argue over the timescales but we are approaching a critical situation that will seriously affect the whole of the people on earth.

There are thus two issues: firstly the real value of energy produced locally from sustainable and renewable resources in relation to the value of energy derived from hydrocarbon fuel. The second is the production and subsequent use of hydrocarbon fuel which creates the damaging effects on the planet to the cost of every individual on the planet but without any restriction or financial price paid for this damage.

As far as the first issue is concerned the UK government has arbitrarily agreed to pay twice the current price for energy supplied for the new proposed nuclear plants to be built in the UK. This is frankly unrealistic because the de-commissioning cost of a reactor is the same as the initial construction cost so this premium is in reality more than a four fold overage payment.

There is however a rational justification for renewable and sustainable energy to be valued at between 1.5 and 2 times centralised energy production based simply on the savings achieved by avoiding transmit ion losses and then a bonus for not destroying the planet.

As far as the second issue is concerned then there needs to be a cost attached to the production and extraction of all hydrocarbon fuels and this needs to account for the damage caused by these fuels when used. This affects everyone on the planet and must be a global agreement by every nation but clearly those who are major producers will be, understandably, not enthusiastic to make payments out of their income. A consensus is thus required where all nations, both consumers and producers, accept a charge against all hydrocarbon fuel that takes some account of the damage this is causing to the world.

It would be impossible to make this charge at point of consumption and it must be calculated and charged at the point of extraction. Equally is appears impossible to determine any recipient of this charge that would be acceptable to the rest. The only possible option, that has any legs at all, is an agreed nominal charge of say 0.05$ per KWh on all extracted hydrocarbon fuel that is essentially paid to the World Bank. This initial charge should be expected to increase over time. Even this would be unacceptable and impossible to agree unless the allocation of these funds was clearly pre-described and definitive. Equally each and every producer must have the option to re-invest their liability, at least in part, in their own environment and in renewable energy systems.

In essence the effect would be for Hydrocarbon producers to pay for the replacement of their output by converting the world to a renewable and sustainable energy system. It could only be accepted if all producers were able to offset the current liability at least by 50% by investing this in their own countries. The overall benefit would remain, countries such as the UK who are both producers and global purchasers, would essentially be in the situation where they are forced to invest into sustainable energy sources in proportion to their hydrocarbon imports thereby elimination the need to import.

The fact is simple, all countries that import energy run a balance of payments deficit, and simplistically wealth created within the country is sent outside the country thereby leaving a shortfall within. The change to sustainable and locally generated energy eliminates this exit of funds and enables each closed environment to become independent and self sustaining.

This applies to every system whether this is a country or a single farmer, if the farmer can create the energy needed to work the farm then he does not need to expend funds to purchase this energy.

Reverting to cheap Chinese steel currently flooding the world this is a combined result of apparently free hydrocarbon fuel, in the form of coal available within China, together with the reduced labour costs within the country. The reduced labour costs are directly related to the average daily consumption of energy, which can be assessed in China, if you discount the proportion of the population still existing at subsistence levels, at about 20 KWh per person per day. In simple terms the energy usage is less than one fifth of the developed world and so the employment costs are proportionally reduced. The problem faced by developing countries is that as their individual energy consumption rises they become less competitive.

The identical assessment of energy usage explains and causes the current problems with displaced people which are the cause of the migration crises currently evident world wide. This migration is towards societies where the energy consumption per capita is higher, this starts in subsistence rural communities with movement to Towns and Cities and then progresses to international movement.

Equally employment costs are proportional to and a function of energy usage per capita so justifying low labour costs.

The corollary is that as energy consumption tends to equalise across the world then the volume of goods shipped will fall as the cost of production in each geographical area moves towards equality with more distant areas. In effect trade will become more localised into substantial population groups, between 500 million to 1 billion people, with significantly limited trade outside each area. If the developed areas can cut their consumption to around 40 KWh per person as the developing countries move above 20KWh then the trade in manufactured goods will effectively cease. The result will be a series of continents with substantial and sustainable internal markets that have very limited external trade in manufactured goods.

If a hydrocarbon extraction tax could be accepted then these funds need to be utilised to provide additional energy to the poorest communities. The provision of just 2KWh per person would make a radical difference as this would both make it possible to provide pumped water and energy for food preparation. The availability of water would not only be a health benefit but would ensure that sufficient crops could be grown thereby moving these to an average consumption of 4KWh per day. The provision of cooking energy would eliminate the need for biomass fuel thereby allowing trees and shrubs to re-grow thus improving the environment and soil stability.

This level of energy could be provided to a community of fifty with solar panels 6m by 10m or by a small hydro generator or wind turbine. It is however essential that this improvement in quality of health and lifestyle does not result in a swift rise in local population which would simply reverse the benefit of the energy provided.

In the developed countries the problem is equally serious but the essential move must be to remove the violent discrepancy between usage and consumption. This requires a change from low efficiency energy use to highly efficient usage, in simplistic terms a move from hydrocarbon fuel to electricity and hydrogen. This can only be achieved if electricity is utilised for most transport and generated locally and by renewable sustainable systems, plus all surplus generated power is converted and stored by efficient electrolysis to hydrogen gas.

A clear commitment to implement this is required and this needs to be accepted both as a clear objective by government policy and by the majority of the population. The financial cost of this conversion is massive, in the order of the whole of the current level of national debt, but this is repayable from the savings both on an individual basis and on a national basis. In the short term the resultant boost to the economy from the capital expenditure in generating systems and local infrastructure enhancements would result in a dramatic rise in overall GDP. Under the current system of estimating economic health, this will be positive step for stability and even provide Governments with flexibility in their expenditure.

This capital expenditure will be funded, in the main, by increased debt to be repaid over a ten year period from the value of the energy generated both for individuals and localised communities. However as these debts are repaid there will be a steady and dramatic reduction in overall GDP due to the combination of reduced overall consumption due to energy efficiency improvements together with individual usage being provided by individual production. In effect the sole part of individual production that will form part of overall GDP will be any surplus sold but not their actual usage.

The net result would be an initial dramatic increase in GDP followed by a steady reduction in GDP from its initial level down to around half over a ten year period. Under the current economic assessment criteria this would imply a drastic and extensive depression despite the reality that during this period the economy would clearly become stronger and more stable.

Renewable systems have the advantage that their lifespan is in excess of seventy five years. This is fundamental to the provision of sustainable energy systems as there is no requirement to depreciate the initial capital investment at all or over short timescales.

If solar systems are considered the panels will operate at almost full rated power for in excess of seventy five years and although some of the control equipment will need maintenance or replacement every decade or so there is a limited requirement to depreciate or amortise the initial investment. The replacement of the capital employed in the installation still needs to be repaid but this can be funded from the income, or the value of the energy savings, produced by the system in typically a ten year period.

The same is true of all free flow generating plant and, although the generators in tidal, hydro and wind turbines will require serious maintenance or renovation within a ten year period; the infrastructure of these will have a lifespan of over seventy five years. The basic realistic calculation for these systems require a depreciation of approximately 33% of the initial cost over 10 years but no depreciation on the balance.

The effect of these is dramatic so that the whole of the additional funds required can be repaid over a ten year period but thereafter the benefit and income remains for the following decades.

There are fundamental queries that need to be determined by government policy such as whether VAT should be charged on all and any investment in renewable energy or for that matter energy saving investment. This VAT charge simply increased the cost by 20% for no real purpose.

It is accepted that when a property is purchased then there is no justification to depreciate the asset purchased simply because its lifespan is around seventy five years and to provide for depreciation is considered abnormal. In reality most property purchasers expect the value of their investment to rise over time rather than to depreciate. The same logical argument applies to renewable energy systems with equivalent life expectancy.

In the same vane each individual is required to maximise their individual investment in renewable energy, at a time when the economy is certainly questionable, so it requires specific government supported loans to be available to all. These loans can be repaid over a 10 year period but need to be secured as additional "energy" borrowing against every suitable property but independent and separate from the existing loans for both home owners and investors. It is also paramount that these loans are transferable on sale and repaid from the income derived from the investment. These loans can be made available to individuals, companies but importantly farmers, who have the possibility to return to their historic position of being both food producers and energy providers.

Currently personal transport, and localised commercial transport, accounts for the majority of pollution in urban areas and consumes a major part of the hydrocarbon fuel usage in developed society. A planned and structured move to electric vehicles would eliminate the pollution and improve energy usage efficiency from the current levels of below 50% to close to 90%. In order to achieve this, fiscal changes would be needed to make the conversion financially attractive. These range from an adjustment to Vehicle Licensing charges and new vehicle tax, these could make new electric or full hybrid rechargeable vehicles both lower in cost to purchase and lower in cost to operate. If this was augmented by a planned and consistent rise in hydrocarbon fuel costs then a radical change in vehicle usage could be achieved over a short timescale. The restriction of hydrocarbon fuelled vehicles from town centres can also be enhanced by tighter congestion charges that are adjusted to prevent the use of all polluting vehicles from urban areas but these have to be phased with the use and availability of new vehicles.

There would be violent and pressurised objections from the current fuel producers and suppliers as well as vehicle manufacturers who have invested heavily in current vehicle production. However Government has a duty to adjust fiscal policy for the benefit of the economy and the population in general so these changes can be justified. The pressure that is exerted on governments by industry cannot be underestimated and it would take committed and determined policy makers to overcome these pressures.

If the average energy consumption figure is acknowledged and it is accepted that there is a direct link between average energy consumption and the overall cost of living then two factors become apparent. Firstly the average income in any society can be adjusted to balance the average energy consumption, so if consumption is reduced by over 50% then in theory it should be possible to reduce all income payments by a similar percentage. Alternatively if energy consumption is cut by 50%

but energy prices are allowed or forced to double within the same timescale then incomes can remain static.

This provides a dramatic opportunity within all developed societies to adjust both the fiscal structure and the lower end of incomes so that the people at the lower end of the income ladder gain proportionately more from the changes. This would require a structured plan of both fiscal changes to the level at which tax is paid combined with a commitment to raise all benefit payments so that during and at the end of the process more funds were made available to the poorer sections of society. This inherently requires a committed government with an overall policy that has clearly defined objectives and a clear pathway to their achievement.

In order to mitigate the environmental damage currently happening and to change the overall energy supply it is realistically necessary for a dramatic and determined change in government policy and objectives. Individuals can follow this path by personal determination and commitment but only those who already have access to finance and facilities. If there is to be a radical change in energy generation then this will require massive funds to be made available and this can only be achieved over a short timescale with full and committed government support. But these new systems have to be locally based and managed so central government is supposed to support a change to the system that will in the long term destroy their own power and authority.

The conflict is abundantly clear, and is further compounded by the existing major multi-national players who will certainly not wish to see a society moving to local control and production thereby making their existing businesses models irrelevant. Politicians only consider the future in time periods defined by the next election but these changes require a long term plan over a twenty year span so a genuine change is required.

Chapter 10
The End—*Or the beginning*

The essential question is whether the problems developed by human activity can be reversed and whether society can evolve to sustainable and balanced systems that do not reduce the standard of living of the overall population. If changes involve a reduction in standard of living then these changes will simply not happen.

Society in the developed world has three fundamental problems to face:

Firstly Climate change will affect everyone on the planet by rising sea levels and by violent changes in climatic conditions. These will cause increased flooding and structural damage to infrastructure as a direct result of increased storms and damaging weather. The damage in the winter of 2015/16 in the UK is estimated to have cost £5 Billion in insurance claims and on top of this there is the basic damage to uninsured infrastructure. The overall effect on global food supplies has been limited to date but if the weather continues to become more violent and extreme and this is combined with an overall rise in sea levels will result in food production being dramatically reduced.

Climatologists now understand that measurable changes in climatic warming are deferred by ten years from the point in time when the pollution occurs. The developed world entered its phase of meteoric increase in energy consumption from 1960 eventually reaching a plateau by 1990, a mere thirty years. The effect of the resultant pollution has been measured as a significant rise in global average temperature following the turn of the century. The developing continents of China, India and the Pacific Rim will increase total pollution levels by a factor of three; this will be over the same short timescale of about thirty years starting around 1990.

The agreed measured rise in global temperatures in 2105 (but measured at the end of 2014) is 1 degree and with the pollution already in place this is likely to increase in the next five years to in excess of 1.5 degrees. This is the critical level calculated by meteorologists that pushes the world's climate into critical and devastating changes. This is likely to occur by 2020 even if pollution stopped miraculously and immediately.

The effects are dramatic. A rise in sea levels of one meter will displace millions of families and make a significant downward change in world food production. A significant increase in periodic and localised rainfall will cause major flooding across all continents causing damage to property. A significant rise in maximum wind speed will cause dramatic damage to infrastructure resulting in loss of power to large sections of society.

Human activity is triggering a global extinction event comparable to the asteroid that killed the dinosaurs and over a time scale that is instantaneous in geological terms. Humans will become part of this extinction event unless the damage is reversed.

Secondly is the effect of global conflict impinging on the societies of the developed world. The reality is that continental Europe is fringed on both its Eastern and Southern boarders by hostility. These conflicts are a mixture of internal civil wars to outright aggression between the super powers of Russia and NATO. These conflicts spread outside the European boarders across Africa and the Middle East to the extent that a major part of the land mass occupied by humans is now in a state of conflict.

These conflicts are affecting life and society within the developed countries by the constant acts of terrorism carried out by individuals who believe that the developed societies act contrary to their religious and social beliefs. This is not to in any way justify these acts of violence but it is essential to comprehend the causes that are the basis behind these views. The indisputable fact is that the developed countries have taken military action across the world in an attempt to control and regulate energy supplies for themselves and these actions have sown the seeds for the conflicts we are seeing today. The developed countries have exercised their economic and military power consistently to their benefit with no regard for the indigenous people or their welfare.

The visible and publicised acts of terrorism have to date been restricted to personal injury on a relatively small scale but it is realistic to assume that these attacks will become even more violent in the future. It is also sensible to assume that these attacks will be targeted at both the financial markets and the fundamental infrastructure of the developed societies. It is now also reasonable to consider a major conflict between the major dominant powers in the world, whether this is Russia verses the West or China verses the rest is rather academic but the foundations for these conflicts are present.

There are currently 65 million displaced persons in the world and the majority of these would move into Continental Europe immediately if they had the opportunity. There are a further billion persons who would also move to the developed world to avoid starvation and conflict. This is the fundamental pressure on migration and the developed world cannot possibly sustain or adsorb this level of migration. N America is protected by two oceans and could easily have a southern wall built, so the USA remains as a vocal supporter of Human Rights but avoids direct involvement.

The only possible solution to this migration pressure is to eliminate the causes at the origin; this would be less expensive in the short term and would avoid the internal pressures within the developed societies. The simple fact is that Europe cannot adsorb even a few million into the current populations so it is essential to reverse the pressure for this migration at source. The developed world must act to provide energy resources to the deprived regions and these will enable those regions to become self sufficient and eventually prosperous.

The link between migration and terrorism is fundamental because both have the same root cause based on fear, aggression and starvation of vast sections of the world population.

Thirdly the developed world economy is totally dependent on current energy supplies, these are limited and will be subject to aggressive price movements in the short term and devastating in the longer term as the limitation on availability becomes apparent. It is clear that OPEC will agree a balance between individual countries production and a fixed rise in the value of crude oil and gas, this is clearly in the interests of all producers and it is simply a matter of time before an agreement is evolved. The simple fact is that all producers would benefit from a global increase in values of their products of 20%+ but the majority producers will not reduce production sufficient to achieve this level of increase whilst faced with the situation where others will simply increase their production to fill demand. This is, however, simply a negotiating position and the benefit to all producers is so apparent that an agreement will be reached quite quickly. The net effect of this agreement will be a hike in crude prices of at least 20% with overall production reduced by less than 10% -- making every producer at least 10% better off and crude prices rising to between $55 and $60 per Barrel.

The effect on the developed economies, who are no longer major producers of these sources of energy, will be dramatic and cause a serious decline in their economies. In the UK this combined with the fall in the value of the pound as a result of the Brexit vote could see overall energy costs rise by over 40% in the short term – this would push the economy into a recession irrespective of any fiscal and support changes made by the government.

However along with these changes the balance of world energy consumption will tend to equalise with the developing societies moving towards the energy consumption of those within the established developed societies. This will have the effect of diminishing the financial benefit of shipping goods half way round the world as the cost of production on a localised level will be lower than the imported cost. In reality this competitive edge for developing countries in money terms can only be sustained if the individuals involved in producing the goods can be forced to have a quality of life that is substandard to their customers. This balancing will simply happen in the longer term so it is a question of timing not the effect that is arguable but unless the whole world modifies its energy use the consequences will be disastrous for all.

Equally if the developed world can move to a substantial reduction in energy consumption then this disparity is further reduced, in essence if the developed societies can reduce their consumption by 50% whilst the developing societies continue to grow their consumption per capita then global trade will be dramatically reduced with more goods produced locally as the transportation costs make movement of goods unrealistic.

The move to a more equalised energy consumption across the globe will invariably lead to a significant reduction in global trade with each large geographical region manufacturing and servicing its own home market with global trade restricted to movement of raw materials and services. In essence the world will become a series of large, and virtually independent, geographical units with limited trade between areas.

The reality is that all developed economies are under strain and only being sustained by national borrowing on an individual and governmental level. This will result in a deep recession, which could well have started in retrospect in 2007, leading to what in effect is a world depression. This will cause chaos in every country and force a financial and monetary re-assessment which will make the current austerity packages seem insignificant and minor, in essence the current economies will collapse.

All three of the above scenarios are fundamentally due to a combination of energy abuse by the developed world and the continuation of the consumption of hydrocarbon fuels by the whole planet. The future can only be positive if a way out of this dependence on hydrocarbon fuel is implemented returning the whole world to a sustainable balanced generation and use of energy.

If the UK purchases £1 million in hydrocarbon fuel the energy is 200 GWh but the energy benefit to the users only amounts to 100GWh due to the inefficiency on combustion. These funds have left the UK at the time of purchase and are not available within the UK economy in the future and once this fuel is used then it has to be purchased again so over a decade over £10 million will have been expended. This remains an ongoing cost indefinitely into the future and any rise in fuel costs will simply increase the annual cost.

Alternatively if £10 million is invested in renewable energy systems then this will provide 32Gwh pa which if valued at 30p per KWh would be £960,000 pa so the initial capital repayment is £800,000. This investment is long term but over an eleven year period assuming an increase in fuel value of just 2.5% pa then the capital is repaid in full and society has the benefit of these 32 GWh for the following decades at negligible cost. This is the problem with renewable sources of energy generation, they are capital based but do all, within a decade, become a source of security and financial stability. This financial stability would return the developed countries to a balanced national budget where expenditure can be based on wealth distribution rather than continual increases in borrowing.

If a printing machine was available that printed authorised Bank of England currency but additionally automatically adjusted the value printed to retain the real value of the currency every year then this would hardly be difficult to sell and have a value of at least twenty times the annual currency printed. This is the dilemma for sustainable energy supplies – the capital investment is high and difficult to achieve but the future becomes positive but every deferment makes the solution harder and more difficult.

The prospect of generating the current consumption of 200 Mtoe within the UK is ni-on impossible from purely sustainable sources and would certainly a monumental objective. But it has to be accepted that a proportion of continued hydrocarbon fuel use will continue simply for long range transport. This is in part to the substantial investment in airbuses and container ships, and also to a lesser extent in long distance haulage transport but this should be contained at less than 10% of current consumption.

This leaves an objective consumption level of around 180 Mtoe and this can be reduced over the next decade by considered population reduction of around 10% and a radical change to a balanced and efficient use of energy at approaching 90% overall against the current level of less than 50% overall. These two would reduce consumption to the order of 80 Mtoe pa – without reducing individual usage and therefore individual standard of living. This is a realistic target for sustainable energy production within the UK and is equally achievable across the developed world. The developing world countries have an easier transition as the changes can be phased in along with the growth in individual usage.

It is paramount that a change back to a sustainable energy environment is implemented. The future needs to be on the basis of energy nodes that provide for local needs that are operated and managed within each community as this eliminates a major part of the current wasted energy. This will provide economic independence and stability to individuals as well the real ability to make choices within each community both for themselves and for the country of which they form a part. But it is essential that the current disparity between consumption and usage is addressed at the same time as this can in itself cut overall consumption by half.

These changes can be implemented by individuals but would be better promoted and encouraged by a central Government policy that adjusts the fiscal environment to press these changes forward in a positive and constructive manner.

There is a frightening similarity to the current world balance with the position that existed in the late 1930's when all aware individuals were conscious of the looming problems but with the politicians avoiding the fundamental issues and burying their heads in rhetoric to avoid taking positive and definitive action. This lead to the 2'nd world war, whereas the current problems could lead to either armed or economic conflict both of which would result in similar devastation across the globe.

The political uncertainty that is apparent is clearly leading to polarisation of national populations with the result that the majority in the middle of the spectrum are in effect unrepresented and disenfranchised and those that do vote are forced to choose the lesser of two evils. This has resulted in various unbelievable electoral results since 2008 but the pinnacle has to be the UK referendum result. The real seriousness of this is probably questionable as although it will undoubtedly cause a recession in the UK and almost certainly within the UE this really does no more than crystallise the underlying problems and simply brings forward the day of reckoning.

These comments are targeted at the UK (and continental Europe) where there is at least a moral responsibility to lead the way forward to a sustainable future, primarily because we started this journey with the industrial use of coal to expand the home economy and develop the Empires. These are now both historic, but in a world that will change as dramatically in the next half century as it has done is the last, then unless steps are taken now all the youngsters on the planet will pay dearly for the excesses of the last fifty years. It is their future, hopefully with the support and commitment of the whole of society, so they will be able to make the changes necessary to have a positive future.